SUPERMARKET DESIGN/1

SUPERMARKET
DESIGN/1

Edited by Martin M. Pegler

Retail Reporting Corp., New York

Retail Reporting Corporation
302 Fifth Avenue
New York, NY 10001

Distributors outside the United States and Canada
Hearst Books International
1350 Avenue of the Americas
New York, NY 10019

Library of Congress Cataloging in Publication Data:
Supermarket Design/1

Printed in Hong Kong
ISBN 0-934590-79-6

Designed: Judy Shepard/Bernard Schleifer

CONTENTS

INTRODUCTION

As we race forward towards the next century and the millennium, we seem to have our eyes fixed on the future. Yet, like the two-faced, Roman god, Janus, we also keep looking back to "the good old days." New supermarkets and hypermarkets are being designed with the newest materials, the latest in technology, and computerized and digitized to the nth degree. However, we still find the designers looking back to the old outdoor, farmer's markets and village squares for inspiration and for the motifs and mementos that will add up to a successful "shopping experience."

It used to be that a market was where one shopped for food necessities, and it was a daily occurrence in urban areas and maybe a weekly affair in the more rural places. It used to be "women's work" and the planning and execution was part of "mother's" full time schedule. Times have changed, people have changed and so have our options. The food and produce presented in the neighborhood markets are no longer the locally provided necessities, but the shopper has choices that come from all over the country — and all over the world. Where we once settled for loaves of prewrapped, waxed paper covered white breads, we now have a wide selection of freshly baked breads, biscuits and muffins to choose from and often they are baked right in the market. Mother no longer has to rush home to make dinner "from scratch"; she, or dad or sis or brother can now pick up all the mixings — all ready to go and beautifully prepared in the deli area of the supermarket. Shopping has become a family affair and one in which the members participate as a group — or alone.

As the reader thumbs through this volume of supermarkets which were culled from all over the U.S., Canada, Latin America, Japan and Europe, he or she will note the designers' emphasis on "the shopping experience" and the need to create a "warm and welcoming" ambience; a store that is "customer friendly."

In order to accomplish this we find wood being used because we associate wood with qualities of "real," "natural" and "wholesome." Lighting is even more important than ever and wherever possible, natural daylight is incorporated into the overall lighting plan. Designers realize the importance of light to create ambience on the products, on the customers and on the perception of the store's image, comfort level and quality. In keeping with the changing times and tastes, colors in supermarket design have changed. They seem to be lighter, gentler, more flattering and easier on the shopper's eyes. White accented with black and natural wood is still a favored combination where a more sophisticated design approach is desired. In every case, the store's lighting does affect the color palette—and how the colors are accepted by the shoppers.

Signage has become, in many instances, the major decorative element in the supermarket design and more and more thought and creative imagination goes into the design and fabrication of these signs. From dimensionalized, polychromed wall plaques that show overscaled products in vibrant color — to stylized neon outlined silhouettes — to the downpour of fabric banners that not only direct the shopper around the vast space but add a feeling of festivity to the hanger-like structures, the graphics, signs and auxiliary signage are carefully designed to promote the store's image as well as the offerings within.

In some cases where a particular ethnic group may be the major shoppers, we find bi-lingual signs added for their comfort and convenience. The graphics can be food oriented but can just as frequently be used to create a sense of "time and place." The graphics and the decorative architectural elements "localize" the space and make it related to the community in which the market is located.

As in every other facet of retailing today, the "Entertainment Factor" must be added. Whether it is the music that fills the air, the animated and flashing signs, the festive settings — they are all there to add "fun" to the shopping experience.

What has become even more pronounced in supermarket design is the food court. More and more markets now provide space for the shoppers to take time out from their shopping to relax, have a snack, a cup of coffee, or just to sample some of the freshly-prepared delicacies — "ready to go." From an in-market, retro diner to a Caribbean or Cuban cafe and all the coffee shops in between —food service in the food courts are here to stay and they are designed to keep the shopper in the market longer.

The supermarkets in this book, as previously stated, are from all over the world and they vary from under 20,000 sq. ft. to over 200,000 sq. ft. There are traditional stores, upscaled gourmet type stores, hypermarkets and local stores. We have included prototypes, renovated spaces, and newly, re-thought classics. We feel that there is a full spectrum of supermarket design treatments in this volume and we hope they will provide information as well as inspiration.

Martin M. Pegler, SVM

SUPERMARKET DESIGN/1

BI-LO

Greenville, South Carolina

This brand new Bi-Lo store of 52,000 sq.ft. was opened in Greenville, South Carolina which happens to be where Bi-Lo Inc. is headquartered. The recently opened facilty —the 195th store in the chain—is actually a new prototype for the company and the design concepts developed by CIP International of Fairfield, Ohio started by completely revamping the configuration of the refrigerated cases and the grocery shelves. It took months of consultation between the Bi-Lo company executives and Thomas Huff and his staff at CIP International to create the new format.

DESIGN:
CIP International, Fairfield, Ohio
Thomas Huff, president and creative director

FOR BI-LO:
Larry Zitzke, V.P. of Construction, Maintenance and Design, Greenville, South Carolina

The hanging, triangular-shaped aisle directory/ pricing signs are part of the comprehensive communication system in the store's design concept.

Neon highlights and large custom graphics are accentuated above eye level to snare the shoppers.

The Deli-Hot Food/Bakery department is located near the store's entrance. It was placed in this conspicuous location because "it makes a wonderful first impression."

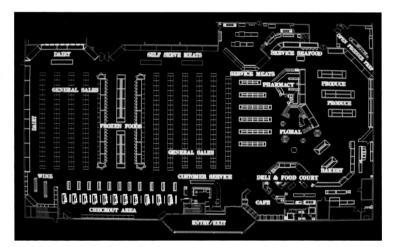

Larry Zitzke, V.P. of Maintenance, Construction and Design for Bi-Lo said, "our operation is geared to meet the needs of the entire community. This store demographically attracts and large segment of the more affluent shoppers." As the accompanying pictures will show, the designers did come up with "an atmosphere conducive to stimulating the consumer to buy groceries and enjoy the shopping experience." The key words to the design process were "stimulating"—"enjoyable" "up-scaled" and, of course, "customer friendly."

In an effort to upscale the overall look of the Bi-Lo store, CIP International suggested the use of wood moulds, trims and ship-laps. These were stained to a rich, deep red mahogany finish. "The classic and updated look was definitely on the design agenda. CIP also created a series of "boutiques" that line up around the central grocery area. The Deli-Hot Food/Bakery department or shop is located near the entrance into the store and it was placed in this conspicuous location because "it makes a wonderful first impression." The sights and smells fill the senses of the incoming shoppers and soon has them wanting more and more of the foods on view. Neon highlights and large custom graphics of pizza, luncheon meats and the delicious baked foods available below are accentuated above eye level to snare the shoppers.

The design firm has also created a complete graphics and signage for Bi-Lo which also includes a "menusystem" which explains daily specials available in the shop and the cost of the items in the cases. Like the hanging, triangular-shaped aisle directory/pricing signs, they are all part of the comprehensive communication system in the store's design concept. In the Seafood/Meat area, the shopper is greeted by a similar graphic display customized for the products sold here. In the Produce area, the wood ship-laps serve as a backdrop for the large artwork graphics of fruits and vegetables.

Three views of "an atmosphere conducive to stimulating the consumer to buy groceries and enjoy the shopping experience."

In the Seafood/Meat area, the shopper is greeted by a similar graphic display customized for the products sold here.

Special "boutique" treatments were also created for the Wine, Floral, and Pharmacy departments. Here is is accomplished by the use of special wall treatments that "create interest and unique drawing cards" for these shops. This added emphasis also highlights these areas to indicate to shoppers that Bi-Lo has much more to offer than just the expected groceries.

The check-out area is treated with a unique ceiling design and with additional accent lamps—"to make a lasting impression."

View of the new Safeway concept with the colorful neon graphics and signage.

SAFEWAY

Peninsula Village, White Rock, BC, Canada

According to the designer of this new prototype Safeway market, "The new concept was to embellish the quality of produce and merchandise through the use of lighting, displays, fixturing and graphics—making this store a special place to shop."

The design is focused on a street market concept within a very large spacial volume of over 50,000 sq. ft. "The interior reflects an "all-in-one' shopping experience with progressive, intimate and friendly ambience." What the designer hoped to achieve on the interior was a "sense of specialness"—with a look and an attitude.

The orientation within is maintained by using "Main Streets" as the most travelled paths in the store—"Secondary Streets" as the perimeter paths and "Pathways" as the aisles. In order for the product to be the main attraction, the major color scheme is neutral and pale. However, each department is made recognizable by the rich, jewel-toned colors used to accentuate it. "Colour is used as an affordable tool to attenuate, enhance and appraise the produce being displayed in each department."

To keep a design continuity between the outside and the inside of the market, the designers utilized architectural elements from the exterior to create patterns that decorate the floor and bulkheads; a square motif within linear bandings. This motif changes color to identify with the department's color scheme and all fixtures used in the department— though standard fixture designs—are customized and specialized with accent colors to match the scheme of the particular department.

DESIGN:
Sunderland Innerspace Design, Inc.,
Vancouver, BC

PHOTOGRAPHY:
Anthony Fulker

A view of the fresh produce department where the neutral color scheme has been accented with deep orange and dark green.

Additional views of the new colorful neon graphics and signage.

The high ceilings were painted white and the overall lighting consists of suspended Holophone fixtures styled to add character to the interior. Accent lighting consists of "market-style" fixtures which theatrically highlight the products. Suspended ceiling grids are also used to identify departments. Feature pendant lights or track lights are attached to the grids which vary in size and shape which conform to the particular department beneath it. "Each grid was left as open as possible to maintain a sense of openness towards the high ceiling throughout the store."

The design intent for this store has set a new precedent for Safeway design standards

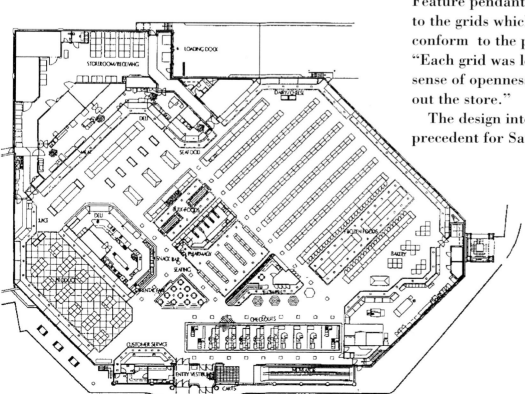

KING KULLEN

Bayshore, NY

P rogrammed Products Corp. was present- ed with a unique challenge when King Kullen Markets invited the designers to enlarge and remodel an existing store in Bayshore. The original 35,000 sq. ft. structure was to be enlarged to 47,500 sq. ft. and the majority of the expansion would be added onto the left side of the space. Many of the small specialty and service shops would have a height of only ten ft., while the rest of the space has a 16 ft. high ceiling. This expansion would create a building greater in width than in depth. The challenge was to design around this "bowling alley" effect and "create archi- tectural depth and interest within the existing build- ing constraints."

The facade of the Bayshore store incorporates King Kullen signature red with a sweeping fan window over the main entrance. The pronounced arch of the roof line introduces the curved lines found within.

Fresh Seafood has aqua and pink tiled walls accented with black and white. It is located near Produce.

Floating graphics with soft, curved lines provide the colorful identification for the Produce department.

DESIGN:
Programmed Products Corp., Plymouth, MI
Llew M. Reszka, President

Sweeping areas of illuminated dropped ceilings serve to highlight special areas of the store.

A new floor plan that best utilized the lowered ceiling was evolved. The solution was "a long, curved secondary ceiling soffit which was designed to blend the old and new structures architecturally." This central soffit not only divided the store into three major areas, it visually balanced the right and left spaces of the interior and also created the "illusion of depth." The design directive for the store was to make it upscale—in keeping with the affluent Bayshore community, and make it stand out from the competition.

The "Southwest L.A." color scheme of brighter than sunwashed desert colors shows up on the patterned vinyl tiled floors. Prominent are the pinks, peaches, teals and mauves.

To accomplish this, the design firm relied on an extensive use of neon signage, high contrasting lighting and dramatic architectural treatments.

The shopping experience begins with the Bakery and Deli Court. Here the designers used the curve to include both the department case line-up and to accentuate the repetitive curves in both the overhead lighted ceiling and the planter box displays. Produce is both highlighted and identified by the floating photo-graphics.

A space frame with a more classic design carries the neon signage over the salad island in the Produce department.

Humor, style and tongue-in-cheek sophistication produced the clever signage: "Lettuce Entertain You" (Produce), "Poultry Pavilion" (chicken & chicken parts), and "Back to Beef" (for the meat area way in the back).

The color scheme is "Southwest Los Angeles." It is bright and lively. Soft peach and sand tones are accented with teals, violets and rose colors. Greenery is evident everywhere. "The effect of this amphitheater combines both architecture and product display which reinforces the positive shopping experience."

The design also reaffirmed King Kullen Markets as a quality and service leader and a place where there is an emphasis on the value of entertainment in the shopping experience.

Clever, tongue-in-cheek sayings are used to identify specific areas such as the "Back to Beef" sign for the meat shop located way in the back of the supermarket.

The checkout area is easily located and the numerous stations are identified by the arched illuminated ceiling with the neon accented number.

GIANT EAGLE

Erie, PA

Not a prototype—but a one-of-a-kind design—was created by PPC for a franchisee with a long-time relationship with the Giant Eagle chain. The general floor plan and the merchandise assortment are similar to those used in traditional Giant Eagle supermarkets, but Joe Zegarelli, the owner of the Erie store, "was looking for something different to complement the product." "The objective," said Llew Reszka, president of the design firm PPC, "was to create an upscale environment using bright colors and a consistent style of graphics to highlight the various departments."

The store was built with a 14 ft. lay-in ceiling throughout and with Giant Eagle's typical recessed one ft. wide continuous fluorescent lighting. The flooring was VCT—and patterned to direct traffic.

The wide white fascia of Giant Eagle's facade is boldly signed in red to set the supermarket apart from the other brick buildings around it.

The store's signature colors are used in the pattern on the floor. Shown here is Frozen Foods.

Ambient light from the one ft. wide fluorescent lighting is typical of most Giant Eagle stores. A deep burgundy stripe outlines the perimeter of the store.

DESIGN:
Programmed Products Corp., Plymouth, MI
Llew M. Reszka, President

FOR GIANT EAGLE/FRANCHISE STORE:
Joe Zegarelli, Owner

An angled, green and white striped "awning" is used on the neutral colored walls. The graphics for the department are contained within a corrugated arch above the angled awning line.

The perimeter walls are neutralized in color—to allow high contrast with the departmental signage. A deep burgundy stripe is painted along the top wall surfaces and at 8 ft. from the floor there is a diamond motif graphic repeated throughout. The signage system consists of an angled wood and batten roof with corrugated arched vaulting over which the colorful and often playful graphics are applied. "Exposed trusses and radiating framework support the roof structures, graphics, and signage, and also provide a lighter, open look."

The perishables departments are organized up front where the shopper can see and smell them upon entering the store. Along the whole exterior wall, the produce is shown with display islands and innovative massing in the middle of the space under the hanging graphic identification. The specialty shops are locat-

ed opposite the Produce: Deli, Chinese and Pizza. They separate this side of the store from the groceries. Meat, Dairy and the Bakery departments surround the remaining perimeter. Frozen Foods is located in the middle aisle and the Pharmacy and Services are positioned opposite the specialty core.

A richly-colored flooring pattern directs traffic around and through the various departments and shops. Up front, at the checkout counters, the strong floor tile pattern reinforces the theme used in the store and a majority of the colors used.

Simple overhead markers indicate the checkout locations and the repetition of graphic signage "constantly informs the customer of merchandise spotted throughout." "The colors and graphics are a complement to the outstanding product presentation and merchandising techniques which are played out."

A closer look at the graphics in the Seafoods & Meats area.

The consistent design of the signage and the color scheme of burgundy and green pull the store's design together. "The color and graphics complement the outstanding produce presentation."

VILLAGE MARKET

Ganges, BC Canada

G anges is a rather special village. It is an artistic community and also the home of many out-of-doors activities. There is an emphasis here on hand-crafted things as well as on the preservation of nature. King Design International was called upon by Robert Large, the owner of Village Market, to give a "cosmetic facelift" to his 20,000 sq. ft. store. It was a traditional 1970s style supermarket and the client wanted "a clean and fresh look" that would capture the uniqueness of the area's clientele. Specifically, Robert Large wanted to reinforce his—and his store's—involvement in the community and the local history.

DESIGN:
King Design International, Eugene, OR

MARKETING & DESIGN TEAM:
Trevor Burton/Christopher Studach

PHOTOGRAPHER:
John Thompson, Victoria, BC

The natural woods and gentle earth tones are used in the Produce area and elsewhere in the store to "create a fresh and natural feeling."

Pendant metal lamp shades with warm incandescent lamps are suspended over the island display areas. Historical photos of the community and of long gone products and packaging are used to decorate the perimeter walls.

The dusty blue fascia continues around the perimeter wall highlighted with the illuminated "old-fashioned" pictures.

"Nuts & Grains" shares the natural wood planked fascia with the other specialty shops located along the walls.

The designers suggested and instituted a palette of light woods and soft earth tones to "create a fresh and natural feeling" throughout the store. These colors and materials were applied to wall surfaces, the case skirtings, and even used for the graphics and signage—for a very complete visual appearance. Historical photographs of the local area and of old time products and packaging were framed and used to highlight areas around the perimeter of the store. They help to convey the store's involvement in the community and also express a sense of pride in work and product. The designers came up with special markers at the checkout stands with short phrases that are meant to impress the store's attitudes, standards and ethics.

All this—together with the new color palette—"reinforced the sense of community pride and long-standing association in the area."

The checkout area is identified with messages that are meant to impress the customer with the store's image, standards and ethics. These statements, along with the palette and the decor elements, "reinforce the sense of community pride and longstanding association in this area."

The signage is simple, bold and consistent throughout the market.

BRUNO'S FOODMAX SUPERCENTER

Lake City, GA

Bruno's is Alabama's largest supermarket chain with five separate store formats. Each group has its own identity, its own decor program and therefore Bruno's can usually move into almost any demographic market. This almost 60,000 sq. ft. store was built in Georgia—which is outside of Bruno's usual "stronghold" and the design concept that was approved is "an open marketplace environment." "Each department was to have its own separate identity and flavor and the customers were to feel as though they were walking past individual shops."

The Foodmax Supercenter facade is finished in a sophisticated color scheme of burgundy, gray, black and white. The specialty areas within are highlighted in white on the deep red band that wraps around the building.

The open beam and lattice ceiling allows natural light to spill in from the clerestory glass in the store's front wall. The light color also enhances the open, out-of-doors feeling.

The "open marketplace environment" is immediately perceived in Produce. A hanging trellis is suspended over the central Produce area and the planter boxes that cap the trellis pour over with silk foliage.

DESIGN:
Programmed Products Corp., Plymouth, MI
Llew M. Reszka, President

ARCHITECTS:
The Garrison-Barrett Group Architects, Birmingham, AL
TWH Architects

GENERAL CONTRACTOR:
Boatner Construction, Gadsden, AL

CEILINGS:
ALL EXPOSED OPEN CELL CEILINGS:
Alcan Ceiling System

LIGHTING:
Lithonia HID with Acrylic Dome

FLOORING:
VCT, Armstrong

STAMPED CONCRETE:
Specialty Concrete Co., San Antonio, TX

FIXTURES:
Metal Gondolas by Madix

MILLWORK & CUSTOM FIXTURES:
Southern Store Fixtures

The Pizza & Cheese shop has its own "building" out on the floor. The multi-angled roof is finished with simulated terra cotta tiles and complemented by the dark green stained woods. The 19th century ambience is reinforced by the old lamp post, the bushels and baskets and the simple, natural slatted wood tables set around the "building."

Shoppers can enter from either end of the building. The customer is "drawn" to the right side of the building where store fronts and roof structures are visible in "a welcoming atmosphere." Here the shopper starts on a journey for a special shopping experience.

The exposed ceiling, which carries the HID lighting as well as the mechanical and construction elements, is painted a soft, pastel yellow. The perimeter floor is concrete—stamped with a wood plank pattern set at a 45 degree angle to the perimeter walls. This lends "an authentic farmers' market/open air flavor to the space."

A roof structure covers the Floral Shop which, with the Produce department, becomes "the benchmark of the overall atmosphere." The open beam and lattice ceiling allows natural light to penetrate from the clerestory glass at the front wall.

Old fashioned street lamps, planked "wood floors," basket and such add charm and flavor to the Bakery & Cafe area.

Farm and barn architectural elements are dimensionally applied on the perimeter wall in the Seafoods and Meats areas. Applied moldings, window frames, tiled roofs and other building textures add interest to the composition as well as shadows. The diagonally laid wood planked floor continues here.

Architectural moldings, pseudo windows and handsome graphics combine to create the unique atmosphere of Foodmax.

A hanging trellis is suspended over the central open produce prep area and planter boxes with artificial foliage surround the trellis. Fabric banners are suspended between the trusses and fabric awnings are mounted over the perimeter produce cases "to soften the hard line of the cases." Custom European flower carts, Barcelona carts and produce platforms are used throughout the area to display the merchandise in a colorful and atmospheric manner.

The Pizza and Cheese island has its own separate roof structure with simulated terra cotta roof tiles. The Bakery and Deli—opposite—are detailed with architectural pediment signage.

False windows with simulated sky and clouds beyond adorn the wall surfaces throughout the market. Continuing on the stroll through the open mar-

Frozen Foods. The metal halide lamps in their white glass fixtures are used to achieve the pleasant ambient light in the store.

The green and white striped awning is suspended over the wood wine fixtures. Giant graphics of luscious grapes indicate that this is the Wine department. Seen in the rear is the tiled roof of the Pizza & Cheese shop.

An impressive overhead structure also highlights the checkout counters. A giant Foodmax sign on a lattice wood background is centered in the main arch of the suspended roof. The clerestory windows in the front wall, seen here, allow daylight to permeate throughout the store.

A suspended dropped ceiling—fully illuminated—hangs over the Pharmacy to set it apart as a special service entity in Foodmax. It conforms to the space and shape of the department.

The roof structure over the Floral Shop, up front, becomes "the benchmark of the overall atmosphere." Custom European flower carts, Barcelona carts and "antique" touches make this a one-of-a-kind shop within the store.

ket, the shopper comes upon a storefront reminiscent of a shack on a wharf with built out facade, gabled roof lines and authentic building materials. This is the Seafood specialty shop. Fresh Meats are sold in multi-deck cases set under a cedar shake roof/awning. As mentioned, architectural moldings, pseudo windows and handsome graphics all combine to add to the ambience of this Foodmax.

Near the checkout area are the Pharmacy and Cosmetics department. A roof structure, mounted to a suspended drop wall, conforms to the space and shape of the department. The ceiling system within is an open cell beam grid "which creates a level of comfort and intimacy while allowing natural light to penetrate from the clerestory windows." Even the checkout is highlighted by an impressive overhead structure.

CHIEF FESTIVE FOODS

North Defiance, OH

hief Festive Foods is an Ohio chain of over a dozen supermarkets and the company recently took over a 40,000 sq. ft. store. It was completely renovated by DFI of Troy, MI. The new store is located directly across the street from a new "Super K" store.

In addition to the traditional and specialty foods to be found in a supermarket, the Chief Festive Foods in North Defiance features a "Party Center" which is located up front in the store and sort of serves as a hub for the other departments. This new "concept" area includes everything needed for the planning of special functions from weddings, anniversaries and special birthdays to business meetings and open houses. Besides the balloons, greeting cards, paper goods and the rental of tables, chairs and dishes,

Festive Foods—in bright, multi-colored letters—is splashed across the already colorful facade. Arched rooflines and quarter round yellow "canopies" add a rhythmic quality to the otherwise boxy, brick building.

The Bakery features black faced fixtures and a wood specialty table. The fascia is banded in assorted colors with applied letters and graphics. The mauve color that is used in the departmental signage is also used as an accent stripe on the floor. Rose is another accent color.

Angled black trimmed wood displayers show off the produce on the floor boxed off in a giant grid. The dropped acoustical ceiling is patterned with diffused fluorescent fixtures that provide the ambient light for the space.

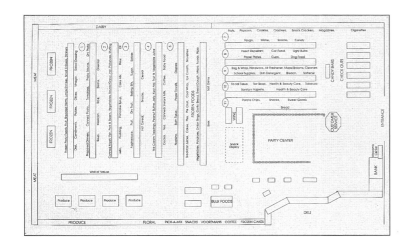

there is a professional planner available to provide guidance and suggestions. In addition, the supermarket has a full service bank branch, and a post office. The new store certainly makes "one stop shopping" a reality.

As a complement to the Party Planning area, the Bakery now features a state-of-the-art, computerized cake decorating machine which allows customers to have "photographs" "airbrushed" onto the cake. The height of personalized trimming! The Deli department, naturally, also lies near the Party Planning department.

DESIGN:
Design Fabrications Inc., Troy, MI

The same look continues in Quality Meats except here a red stripe enlivens the black and chrome refrigerated cases.

The Delicatessen.

In the Grocery part of the store, the "festival" again takes over in the same colorful way that it appears on the facade.

An important part of the Chief store is the Party Express where a shopper can pick up anything and everything to do with having a small dinner party—to a barbeque—to a big wedding reception. Glowing on the left are the neon logos for the beers available adjacent to this Party area.

The store is basically neutral in color with black predominant for the cases and the fixtures, some natural woods and off-white perimeter fascias banded and accented in rose and mauve. "The black cases give a sophisticated look and offer a high contrast background to the display product." The slightly muted palette of accent colors was carefully chosen "to include as many colors as possible without becoming overbearing or confusing the shopper." The whole floor looks like a party is about to happen.

BIG Y WORLD CLASS MARKET

Springfield, MA

This relatively recent 34,300 sq. ft. super-market was built in Springfield, MA as the latest addition to the Big Y Supermarket chain of 30 stores. It was also designed to be the new prototype for the regional chain and meant to show off an "attractive and high-ly service-oriented store with an international flavor; offering specialty shops with specialty foods." Big Y intends to expand their market to include such cus-tomer amenities as a laundry, bank, photo develop-ing service, UPS, Western Union, and a "Green Room" for recycling a variety of products.

The entrance into Big Y is distinguished by the peaked roof over the main entrance as well as the bright logo.

The International Delicatessen is one of the specialty shops to be found around the perimeter of the 34,300 sq. ft. store.

The Produce area. Here the lighting in the 11" ceiling is softer and the diagonal patterned floor can be seen to good advantage.

DESIGN:
Sumner & Schein, Cambridge, MA

The main entrance into the store is designed on a larger scale and thus helps direct the customers from the parking lot — and then along a path which provides the most exposure to all the departments throughout the store. The designers arranged the specialty shops along the perimeter of the store with the general grocery aisles in the center under a 14 ft. raised ceiling. The lowered 11 ft. ceiling, over the specialty shops on the perimeter, makes them appear more intimate and atmospheric.

The customer's journey begins at the "Power Alley" — an open market space featuring specialty departments each with its own theme. There is a bakery with a glass-walled room where a French pastry chef demonstrates his baking skills; a florist, an international delicatessen, pizzeria, and a juice bar and cafe. This area is separated from the circulation zone by lush indoor plantings.

International Foods International Foods
Italian   Kosher Foods
Portuguese   Asian Foods
Greek   Spanish Foods
Jamaican   Mexican

The international theme continues even in the grocery area where the 14 ft. ceiling filled with exposed fluorescent strip lighting. The banners add a festive quality to the otherwise utilitarian space.

Other perimeter shops or departments include: produce, meat/poultry, seafood, dairy, frozen foods, and a "wholesale club."

The materials used are low-maintenance, durable, low cost and attractive. The flooring is VCT but the design resembles porcelain tile and the use of a diagonal pattern creates the impression that the grocery aisles are shorter in length — and that the customer "has the perception of travelling less distance through the store." Uniform rows of exposed fluorescent strips provide efficient illumination over the grocery area.

To add to the international flavor, a wall was designed for "the newspapers of the world" featuring print material from all over the globe as well as a collection of clocks showing the different times around the world.

The Juice Bar & Cafe: two other special amenities in this new-look store.

The special "international" featured wall with newspapers from around the world and clocks showing the time in other parts of the globe.

FRIEDMAN'S BI-LO

Butler, PA

A long piece of history—the history of western Pennsylvania—was revealed with the opening of Friedman's Bi-Lo, 55,000 sq. ft. supermarket in Point Plaza, Butler, PA. Jacob Friedman migrated to Pittsburgh, 30 miles from Butler, where he opened his first grocery store in 1918. In 1949 he opened his first food operation in Butler. At that time it was described as "one of the most modern food markets in Butler." Recently this new Bi-Lo store opened and it is the "most up-to-date, state-of-the-art" supermarket in Butler. However, it still prides itself on being warm, friendly and customer concerned. It is part of the neighborhood.

In this food market customers can buy groceries, rent a movie (from over 5,000 titles), get film developed, pick up some fresh flowers, bring in the cleaning—or just take a relaxing break in the Cafe or find some more exciting amusement in the game arcade. Carole Bitter, Chairperson of Warehouse Foods, Inc. and owner of Bi-Lo says, "We want to make sure a big store isn't cold and unfriendly. This store is pretty near perfect as far as layout because we planned it to death with efficiencies and customer service." She also says, "I'm so excited about this store from a customer's standpoint."

To make sure that all this came true, Bi-Lo worked closely with Design Fabrications, Inc. to create this

The checkerboard band becomes part of the signage in the Fruits & Vegetables area. A white open grid ceiling hangs from the dark green deck roof and metal halides light up the space.

Light natural wood, dark green and white dominate in the Produce area. The checkerboard motif appears as part of the unifying design of the space along with the colorful graphics that highlight each department.

DESIGN:
Design Fabrications, Inc., Troy, MI

The color palette of the store is clean and fresh: white, beige, yellow and green. It is evident in the checkout area where the store's policy sign carries through the color scheme with an accent of red.

A close-up on the Juice area in Produce.

The dark green band separates the sand color below from the white area above. "A billowing ribbon" serves as the unifying signage element throughout. The yellow and green outlines on the white "ribbon" are highlighted with red.

store. The Deli-Bakery service islands separate the conventional value-oriented sales area from the Food Court. The Food Court combines the feeling of a local produce stand with that of an "international food emporium" and together they restate the store's "tradition of service" in this community.

The interior colors are white, beige, yellow and green. The roof deck above is painted a dark green and an open grid mask defines the ceiling plane. Hanging from the grid are large banners and assorted signage—all to "help the eye survey the spaces and provide direction." To create a more personal proportion for the service areas, awnings, flowering rain gutters and billboard type light brackets are added in the specialty shops.

Metal halides provide the general lighting and the lighted perimeter ceiling in the grocery department keeps the open strip lighting from overpowering "the billowing ribbons and lively wall graphics that are tied together by a horizontal band of paint, checkerboard and wood." At eye level, a secondary band on the oak case cornice provides pricing information. The designers used brightly colored floor tiles to complement the light beige cases— "providing a colorful dynamic path as one moves about the store."

Yellow and white striped awnings, rain gutters with foliage and
billboard type light brackets on the curtain wall help to create
a "more personal proportion" for the service area.

THRIFTY FOODS

Broadmead Village, Victoria, BC Canada

This award-winning supermarket of 35,000 sq. ft. was designed for Alex Campbell by King Design International. The design firm researched the neighborhood before settling on the design concept. Though it is an affluent area, the people who live and shop here are also much involved with the environment and things "natural." As for Alex Campbell, the owner of the market, he wanted a store that was "simple, clean and warm in appearance." To accomplish the desired results and satisfy the demographics of the community, the design team created a new layout and a "warm and friendly" color and materials palette.

The "warm and friendly" atmosphere is reflected in the warm, earthy colors and materials. Latticework is "traditional" in this part of British Columbia and the designers incorporated that material into the perimeter wall decor and the signage. The Produce area is also enhanced with old-fashioned fruit crate graphics and striped canvas awnings.

Here, the Pizza and Deli shops—located up front in the store's layout—give the shoppers a sensual hint of what is yet to come.

DESIGN:
King Design International, Eugene, OR

MARKETING & DESIGN TEAM:
Trevor Burton/Christopher Studach/Michael Hopper

ARCHITECT:
Waisman, Dewar, Degrout

PHOTOGRAPHER:
John Thompson, Victoria, BC

The store's new layout places a Deli island up front—near the entry. It provides the incoming shoppers with "a taste of the service-oriented shopping that is to come." In addition to the soft, restful colors, striped awnings were introduced to accentuate the service areas and the specialty stores along with the custom hanging "pub" signs. Just as latticework is a traditional material for this community, the designers incorporated latticework panels into the store's design program.

The gentle, relaxed overall ambience not only enhances the "service" element of the Thrifty Foods image, it also seems to make the shoppers stay longer and shop more.

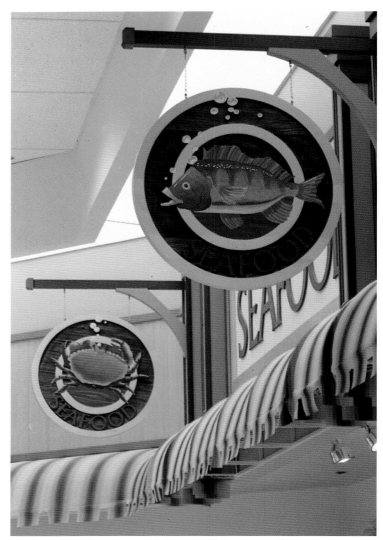

A closer look at one of the "pub"-signs which was used by the designers to further the "part-of-the-community" look of the store.

The Pasta Shop. The illuminated light trough around the island specialty shop helps to give it extra prominence on the floor. An illuminated ceiling, under the fascia, bathes the merchandise and products with warm light.

In addition to the arched green and white awnings over the specialty shops, "pub"-style signs set at right angles to the wall are used to "illustrate" what is available below.

RAY'S SIGNATURE FOODS

Lima, OH

In the new Ray's Signature Foods in Lima, OH, 25,000 sq. ft. of the total 30,000 sq. ft. is devoted to the sale of food. Basically, the designers at Design Fabrications, Inc. used a simple and classic palette of natural oak complemented with the richness of brass in an otherwise striking black and white setting. Added to this is "the warm glow of neon, and the sparkle of incandescent light" which, in turn, helps to add some warmth and charm to the earthtone floor tiles and the ceramic accents used throughout the store.

The diagonal floor tile pattern in the Deli department "creates a dynamic flow to the traffic circula-

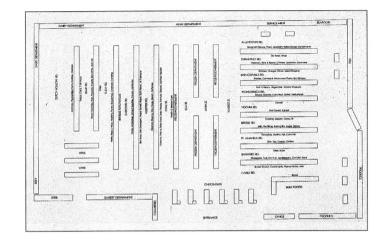

The Butcher Shop: wood slats (like butcher-block) become the background for the raised brass-toned letters and the neon highlighted graphic of the product. Gray, blue and white is the basic cool color scheme upon which bright decorative colors and neon accents are overlaid.

Bright ultramarine blue tiles cover the back walls of the specialty shops that are lined up under the dropped wood fascia which carries the product offerings. Dropped pendant, half-ball lamps bring attention to the merchandise presented below.

The contemporary, textured gray stone facade is complemented by the sophisticated signage applied over it.

DESIGN:
Design Fabrications Inc., Troy, MI

tion" which seems to carry the shopper through the space. Special decorative details and elements were used in the perimeter shops to identify and separate one from the other. One example is the elegant though oversized "bay window" fashioned out of brass tubing with neon letters superimposed on an oak background. This creates a rather special look for the Fresh Meats department.

A very important part of the total design is the lighting plan. DFI specified that the painted perimeter ceiling be bounded by aluminum light baffles. Recessed deep cell HID troffers are used "to reduce visual brightness in contrast with the open strip lighting above the centrally-located, main grocery sales area." Low voltage pin spots on stems are used in Produce, Wine and the Bakery areas to "lend a dramatic flair to the merchandise" being presented there.

A long view of the Deli area. An architectural arch with keystone surrounds the neon signage on the natural slatted wood background. The effective use of the pendant lights can be fully appreciated in this view as well as the patterning on the floor in blue, warm gray and white.

Throughout, DFI has endeavored to create an "upscale" look for Ray's Signature Foods—without appearing either pretentious or pompous. Some of the details that add stature to the total design and the market are the "etched" glass panels, the planter boxes, the style and look of the lettering used for the signage, the graphics and the hanging banners that with the signage appear throughout the space.

The arch motif also encloses the Bakery department signage. Here, the blue color is played up and it is complemented with black and white. The HQI track lighting system adds special life and sparkle to the wines stacked on the wood fixtures.

Fresh Meats, in hot pink neon against the vertically slatted wood wall, is decoratively enhanced by a curved brass grid set in front of it. Below, the meats are shown on tiered shelves. Black appears on the bases of the refrigerated cases and it also makes a strong horizontal band over the wall cases.

DELCHAMPS

Airport Blvd., Mobile, AL

The 58,000 sq. ft. flagship store that Delchamps opened in its own hometown, Mobile, AL, is more than a market or supermarket. It is a "convenient shopping experience" as George Waldron, V.P. of Marketing for the 120-store chain proudly announces. In addition to groceries, produce and foods in all degrees of preparation, the one-stop shopping place includes a food court, a pharmacy and a number of special services including a notary public and even a desk where hunting licenses can be procured. "We attempted to create a design that will serve all kinds of people—not just one type of customer," says Waldron.

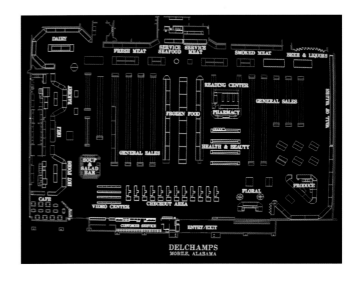

Distinguishing the Delchamps interiors are the colorful and dimensional wall signs and graphics. Here, in Produce, it is the Fruit Store sign. The cases have wood finished bases and the floor is patterned in an overscaled parquet design in beige and white.

A look down the Frozen Foods area. Metal halide lamps, which are energy efficient, are used to illuminate the multi-colored store. The exposed deck roof is painted white.

DESIGN:
CIP International, Fairfield, OH
Thomas Huff, CEO and Creative Director

FIXTURING:
MADIX Corp., Goodwater, AL

LIGHTING:
Abolite, Cincinnati, OH
Halo Lighting, Elk Grove Village, IL
Lithonia Lighting, Lithonia, GA

REFRIGERATION:
Hussman Corp., St. Louis, MO

The beer cooler area is highlighted with a Rathskeller sign decorated with beer steins and a pretzel.

The uniqueness of the design, created by CIP International of Fairfield, OH, starts with the two entrances. One is ideal for the shopper who prefers to shop by walking up and down the aisles while the other "cuts to the chase": it is for the shopper in a hurry who wants quick service.

Thomas Huff, CEO of the design firm, says that the interior "resembles a marketplace or city center of days gone by." The environment says that this is not your everyday kind of supermarket. The areas in the store are differentiated by vinyl flooring tiles that are color coordinated by department. The flooring patterns also direct the shopper from one specialty shop to another.

A close-up on the Bakery signage.

A popular spot in Delchamps is the '50s-inspired Delchamps Diner—part of the store's food court. An art deco/moderne look is captured in the diner's signage and the pink neon complements the design concept.

The Delicatessen area: it is distinguished by the black and white checkered floor pattern and the deep forest green valance over the merchandise presentation. A massive burgundy molding outlines the area and separates the pink-toned wall from the blacked out perimeter wall above. The flooring colors and the department colors are coordinated. Incandescent spots are added to accent the product displays.

In Seafood-Meats, a deep red valance marks off the shop's space and in front, the red and white checkered floor pattern complements the color of the valance. The dimensional sign is in navy, accented with red and gold—plus the rich colors for the rendering of the product.

The Food Court is filled with ethnic food specialties including the popular Wok & Roll Chinese Foods. Each prepared food shop has its own distinctive signage.

The signage and customer information panels are plentiful and many are made of a unique material/process which allows really big and "thick" signs and panels to still be remarkably lightweight. The combination of vacuum formed plastic and high density polyfoam results in a highly dimensionalized, decorative panel which can then be hand painted.

The assorted fresh food products are located along the perimeter walls and they are highlighted by the aforementioned dimensional signs/panels. Canopies, moldings, canvas awnings, and theater marquees add to the overall excitement of the space. Individual shops are set up to showcase freshly-prepared foods and some carry unusual names such as "The Wok & Roll Chinese Food Shop."

The food court is not only a place to shop for prepared foods-to-go, it is an oasis where the shopper can stop, relax over a cup of coffee—or lunch with friends. The court features a full service bakery, deli, hot, salad bar, and a sit-down, art deco themed diner. The "Delchamps Diner" even has a juke box that plays old-fashioned "dance" music.

The Dairy area. The neon cheese explains the products available below.

A theater marquee out of the "good old days" past—sizzling with neon and a back-lighted, illuminated sign board gives special emphasis to this area. This, plus other design details, was incorporated into the total Delchamps design package to make the store seem like "a marketplace or city center of days gone by."

The Pharmacy.

A pink, cerise and white striped, angled "awning-cornice" extends out over the flowers and plants in the Floral Shop. The multi-pink sign steps off the pale pink wall behind it and the rich burgundy moldings that contain the space. The area is separated from the rest of the selling floor by the aqua and white, diagonally-laid, checkerboard pattern.

The checkout stations are identified by arched signs in navy, red and gold. The metal halide lamps are lined up over the counters. Magazines are displayed on the half-round displayer shelves in front of each checkout aisle. The signage colors are repeated in bands on the floor along the front of the checkout area.

To light up the vari-colored interior, energy efficient, metal halide fixtures are used way up overhead in the open ceiling over the general sales area. The lighting plan also calls for some tungsten and halogen fixtures to provide what might simulate a kind of out-of-doors daylight.

This design concept will now be introduced into new Delchamps stores and also adapted where renovations are being planned. George Waldron, speaking for Delchamps says that it is a "fun store" that has really piqued the interest of the community. And—it is convenient!

The bright red Big Bear sign appears on the roughly textured, deep gray, concrete block facade. A peaked roof with a clerestory window breaks the straight roof line.

BIG BEAR

Grove City, OH

The Big Bear supermarket in Grove City is the latest example of store format design for this chain in which the objective was to expand the non-foods departments (toys, appliances, infants & toddlers, softgoods, cosmetics, etc.). In addition to expanding the non-foods, the new plan called for enlarging the frozen foods, deli and butcher shop areas.

The 70,021 sq. ft. store is predominantly colored red, white and gray—and the scheme is quite dramatic. The shopper enters this left-hand layout into a

A white grid space form, outlined in the signature red, is dropped over the grocery area. The aisle signage is in red with white and deep gray with white, while red enameled cornices cap off the gondolas standing on the white vinyl floors.

The same color scheme plus crisp white is carried through inside the store. Here, the Fresh Meats department—along a perimeter wall—has a red and white neon accented department sign across the fascia which is capped with a deep bold red band. The refrigerated cases have matching red enameled bases. A gray and white "flat awning" decorates the lower area. The higher ceilinged area, up front, carries the grocery items.

A blue neon ribbon follows the contours of the bulkhead in the produce department.

DESIGN:
Programmed Products Corp., Plymouth, MI
Llew M. Reszka, President

FOR BIG BEAR:
Stephen Breech, VP Construction/Real Estate

GENERAL CONTRACTOR:
Continental Building Systems

ARCHITECTS:
Richard Trott & Partners, Architects

CEILING SYSTEMS:
Alcan Beam/Cell Ceiling

LIGHTING:
Lithonia, G.E. (Prismatic Fixtures)

MILLWORK/CUSTOM FIXTURES:
Gay & Chaffin, Chillicothe, OH

FIXTURES:
Ontario Store Fixtures.

Some areas of the store have gray and white vertically striped patterns on the soffits over the merchandise. The Seafoods, on the left, are displayed in steel cases against a bright red tiled wall. Overhead, gray and red horizontal bands follow the curved fascia. The signage becomes part of the area's decor and each sign has a curved end to conform with the curve in the wall to which it is attached at right angles.

low ceilinged perimeter. To get to the Bakery and the Deli, the shopper must pass by the Floral and Greeting Cards shops. These two shops are understated in color and decor but a green and purple neon ribbon follows the contours of the bulkhead, and the signing is juxtaposed onto the architectural drops. By design, the signage "disappears" into the ceiling.

A stepped space form accents the Deli area and directly opposite, the glow of uplit, gently-curved photomurals spans the length of the entire bulkhead above the Bakery. "Extraordinary fixtures and merchandising highlight the product and create a most appetizing department."

A curved, formed metal drop becomes the frame for an open celled ceiling system in the Produce area. Its light coloration and sweeping lines of neon all contrast with the dark painted plenum above it. Track lighting provides the illumination that highlights the merchandise displayed below. The repetitive gray and white striping that appears on many perimeter wall shops also is seen here. Above the open produce prep area is the main neon sign for this department.

As the shopper leaves this area, she enters into the part of the store that boasts of a high exposed ceiling structure. Throughout the remaining perimeter space meats, seafood and frozen foods are identified with bold red and white signage with neon used to create the decorative elements. A series of white laminate decor beams are suspended over the wine and frozen foods areas.

In the Bakery area, the back-lit photomurals are gently curved and softly bridge the space from the lowered ceiling to the ceiling of the prep area. White and "gold" trimmed fixtures are used to show off the baked goods.

Frozen Foods has white refrigerated cases accented with red.

To get to the Deli, the shopper passes through the Floral and Greeting Cards shops which are delineated by the purple and green neon ribbons that follow the sweeping curves of the bulkheads above. They are both fixtured mainly in black and identified by the 3/4 round circle motifs in red and white.

The gray and white striped valance and the red signage and accents are complemented by the red/gray/white "plaid" pattern on the floor in the Deli area. The stepped space form hanging down in front also highlights this area.

"This store is dynamic in its stark contrasts and bold graphics. Not only does the decor complement the expertise of Big Bear's merchandise and display techniques, it also creates excitement."

Track lighting on the underside of the beam serves to light up the wine presentation. In Frozen Foods, uplighting over the perimeter reach-in cases illuminates the wall-mounted category signs, and also "tends to expand the space."

Hi-Bay lighting is predominant in the central part of the store—over both food and non-food displays. In the non-food area an open cell space grid is suspended overhead. The light colored grid contrasts with light gray structures above. HID lighting is integrated into the ceiling system in the form of 2 ft. x 2 ft. lay-in fixtures. The entire suspended gridwork is framed by a slick, stepped red gloss laminated cove. The grid is on a 45 degree axis to the gondolas below.

"This store is dynamic in its stark contrasts and bold graphics. Not only does the decor complement the expertise of Big Bear's merchandising and display techniques, it also creates excitement."

L O E B

Bayly St., Ajax, ON Canada

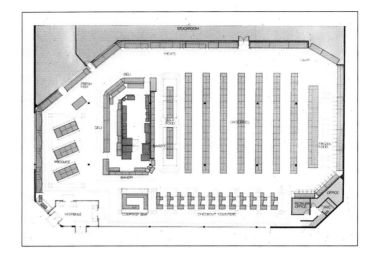

Working with a very limited budget, the design team of International Design Group of Toronto followed the client's directive to "animate the large, high and anonymous space." The design solution that was adopted was to affect a large garden feeling that would somehow permeate through the whole space.

A series of architectural garden elements and motifs were created and used in the store: pergolas, gazebos, latticework panels, arches and planters.

To create an open, out-of-doors, garden feeling—on a limited budget—the designers worked with readily available and relatively inexpensive materials such as trellises and latticework—as well as a palette of white, green and sky blue. White outline arches span over the central area of the market and green garden latticework units from which silk plants are suspended, up front, near the checkout counters.

The sky blue walls suggest the outdoors and the simple white slat constructions add depth and dimension to the setting. The use of the green foliage also recalls the garden setting.

The lattice/trellis combination shows up in the Produce area. The bases of the display cases are covered with diagonal slats of inexpensive lumber which is stained green. Green also appears in the tiled walls of the prep area and as decorative inserts on the white vinyl floors.

DESIGN:
International Design Group, Toronto, ON Canada
Ronald J. Harris/John Shaver

A detail of the mosaic/tile wall in the product area.

Bulk Food. A skeletal, multi-arced arch floats over the center of the space which is highlighted by the green and white patterned floor accented with touches of yellow and copper. Note the "cloud filled blue sky" in the rear. It is part of the Produce department.

A closer look at the arch with the suspended hanging silk plants and the globe lights with the white metal shades.

A gentrified touch: a pair of white wicker chairs and a garden table are set out in the Meat department. A white lattice canopy extends out from the sky-blue wall into a green and white tile checkerboard motif set above the tiers of shelved meats.

The "garden feeling" is also introduced into Dairy.

"Clouds" were painted on the perimeter walls to further suggest the out-of-doors setting. The designers also introduced a floral ceramic tile on the floor and filled the planters with silk plants and flowers.

For the graphics and signage, International Design Group's design team introduced a palette of bright, sunny, flower-fresh colors. The overall "garden" atmosphere with the walks—the garden architecture—the soft, cool, out-of-doors feeling—the sense of openess and light all together resulted in "a warm and friendly atmosphere."

WELTON'S PIGGLY WIGGLY

Gurnee, IL

The Piggly Wiggly chain of supermarkets is well known and readily recognized throughout the southeastern United States and it is rapidly moving westward. To create this 47,000 sq. ft. store, Welton Management Services of Gurnee, IL came to Programmed Products Corp. of Plymouth, MI for a total interior design and decor package. With Llew Reszka, the president of PPC, at the helm the illustrated project was completed.

The facade of Piggly Wiggly

Brightly-colored awnings with and without architectural cornices create an exciting and nostalgic look for this Piggly Wiggly market. In the Produce department, a band of mosaic tiles in white, red and green makes a decorative border for the light green bases of the fixtures. The floor is covered with small tiles detailed with squares of red and green tiles.

The Bakery. A natural pine wood valence accented in raspberry
and burgundy distinguishes this shop. The natural wood is also
used as an accent in fixturing the space. A burgundy and orange
checkered tile pattern makes a shocking band under the plain
wood valence. The same colors appear in the signage.
Incandescent lamps are used to warm up the product display.

DESIGN:
Programmed Products Corp.
Plymouth, MI
Llew M. Reszka, President

OWNER & PRESIDENT:
Richard A. Welton

PROJECT MANAGER:
Gary Elsbury

STORE PLANNING (IN-HOUSE):
Shultz Sav-O-Stores, Sheboygan, WI

Natural pine wood sheathes the fascia wall in the Dairy and here the checkerboard pattern is in green and violet and rich burgundy is the accent color. Green bands finish off the refrigerated cases and a burgundy stripe outlines the perimeter of the department.

Meat Department. Once again, the major colors and material emphasis is on the rich deep green and the natural pine wood. The metal halide lamps are covered with "old-fashioned" pressed glass shades—to add to the "nostalgic" quality of the total design.

Frozen Foods. Variations on a theme: natural pine wood, green, orange, burgundy and striped awnings.

The decor package was conceived by PPC "to set the store apart from the major chain stores by picking up the flavor of the community in which the store was located. In effect, the designers attempted to make this store fit the Gurnee look. This village has a special town section where all the government buildings are located. This area is called "Village Center." Here, old fashioned village lamp posts are used to distinguish the particular place from the rest of the suburban town. Welton's and PPC made use of these lamp posts throughout the interior of the store as well as out in the parking lot to further enhance the "home-town" feeling of this Piggly Wiggly store.

In the Deli-Cafe area, turquoise and white—accented with black—take over, but the recurring burgundy/orange checkerboard motif can still be seen on the perimeter wall.

Pine woods, soft colors and canvas canopies are used decoratively in this supermarket along with raised wood circular elements to further that "down-home" or "country" ambience. The 22 ft. high ceilings allowed the design team to emphasize the individual departments and areas with wooden peaks and special "beams" around the specific areas. A 5 ft. x 60 ft. long mural starts at the front of the store — above the entrance — and it depicts the unique historical past of the Gurnee community. As the designer says, "The many different pictures give the store a unique community-friendly feeling." No doubt, this is a supermarket with a difference — and with a distinctive look that is further enhanced by the graphics program.

A skeletal "roof" of Victorian vintage design floats over the Flower Shop and the space is firmly anchored by the tile border around it.

The checkout area. Old-fashioned lamp posts, typical of those found here, mark off the aqua, beige and black counters. The signage continues with the red and blue seen within the store. The grocery aisle signage is mostly turquoise, deep red, green, beige and black.

STERK'S SUPER FOODS

Whiting, IN

Sterk's Super Foods store is located in a "transitional" blue collar (workers) area in the extreme northwest corner of Indiana. The original "small, tired store" was replaced with a new and stimulating design by DFI of Troy, MI. "Synergy is evident between interior and exterior as the triangular departmental focus mirrors the exterior facade.

This became evident when the original old store was demolished and the parking lot was completed." Bright cool colors and dimensional graphic stripes serve to welcome the shoppers into the "bright, upscale, transitional" store. Focus is on quality, variety, selection and price. Special emphasis has been given to the full, in-store Bakery, Hot Foods, Deli, Seafood and Butcher shops.

Bright colors dominate in Sterk's. Turquoise, green and ultramarine appear over and over again accented with black and white. Here, in Produce, the colors appear in the graphic wall treatment, in the green item signage and the turquoise tiles that are surrounded by white tiles set in the gray floor.

Frozen Foods. The same basic wall treatment is used here though the blues are more prominent in the border patterns on the floor. Blue is also used to trim the refrigerated cases and on the price signage.

DESIGN:
Design Fabrications Inc., Troy, MI

Deli-Bakery. The rear wall is patterned with turquoise and navy on white. A dark purple border on the floor complements the purple stripes and the graphics on the pastel mauve fascia in this area. Neon highlights the stylized, multi-colored product graphics.

The areas are further identified by two inch foam letters overlaid. "The result is a moderate, upscale effect." The flooring in the store is Armstrong's Excellon vinyl tiles which is color compatible with the interior design scheme. The tiles also help to set the "direction"—traffic patterns are set with the tile patterns and colors. Quarry tile, however, is used in the vestibule area.

The lighting has been carefully planned to open up the space since the 22,400 s.f. of sales space (out of a total of 32,500 sq. ft.) is basically narrow and deep. The designers specified Abolite 400 watt metal halide lights at 14 ft. 4 in. to provide the general, overall illumination. Fluorescent case top fixtures provide the wall wash of light. Together they do seem to open up the space.

The deep blue and purple continues in the Butcher shop while Seafoods sparkles with greens, turquoise and light blue.

The blue palette continues into the Floral Shop where red and violet neon burst through the cool ambience to warm up the plants and flowers.

The graphic stepped pediment motif with horizontal lines reappears at Checkout. A purple "Thank You" sends the customers on their way. Here, the first is patterned with assorted pastel blue and white squares.

SUPER MAZ

Valladolid, Yucatan, Mexico

This, the latest of the eight Super Maz supermarkets in Mexico, is the first to be located in a strip center. It is located along a narrow and bustling main street in Valladolid, in the Yucatan, with a court-yard entrance into the 17,000 sq. ft. space. The sales area takes up 78% of the total square footage. The area is rich in Spanish Colonial influences that date back to the 1500s.

To create the "look" for this Super Maz, CIP International researched specific architectural and design elements from the surrounding Spanish

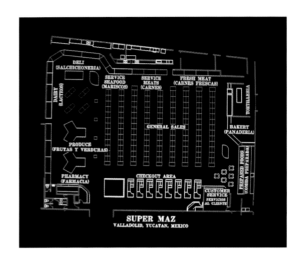

The design and decor elements used in Super Maz, in the Yucatan, are based on historic Spanish Colonial, Mayan and Toltec architecture and art. Here, at the Service Desk, the bold teal border design that borders the fascia is based on a stone design found in a nearby archaeological site.

Spanish Colonial architecture inspired the soft curves and stepped angles in the wall design seen here in Fruits & Vegetables. The palette is soft and muted: mainly aqua, teal, pink, soft coral and mauve along with neutral sand colors. A fuller and brighter palette is reserved for the signage and the graphics.

DESIGN:
CIP International, Fairfield, OH
Thomas Huff, CEO & Creative Director

Colonial, Mayan and Toltec sites and structures—"to ensure a design with local color and demographic appeal."

The open bar joist ceiling construction not only adds to the "open marketplace" atmosphere but it seems to open up the space as well. Metal halides were used to provide the ambient light for the products displayed in the grocery aisles and product oriented light fixtures deliver light temperatures and levels which keep the merchandise in the foreground. Intricate mosaic ceramic patterns are used on the walls while the floor is paved with porcelain tiles. They reinforce Super Maz's emphasis on high quality services and perishables in the prep areas.

Even the "tiled roof" that finishes off this Spanish Colonial facade is soft and muted: a faded, sun-washed dubonnet rather than orange or terra cotta. The deck roof above is painted white and the metal halide lamps are suspended from the ceiling. The upper perimeter walls are painted out a deep gray so that the Spanish Colonial roof line stands away from the wall abetted by the dramatic moldings used.

The decorative motifs used on the interior are a blend of the historic styles mentioned above. "Innovative construction and finishing details portray a Spanish Colonial streetscape below a dark upper wall." There are Spanish style wall letters and a continuous roofing system covered with Spanish terra cotta tiles. Along the perimeter walls, vivid teal accented panels, based on actual stone mosaic patterns from the Palace of Mitla, are decoratively applied. Authentic Mayan hieroglyphic designs, fully dimensional and computer routed, are used to border the departmental wall signage.

A closer look at the Meat & Fish areas. Note the colored tiled walls on the prep area walls and the back lit photos.

Dairy & the Beer Cooler Cases. The bold stepped motif in teal appears against the sandy pale coral wall. Muted deep rose lettering is used here for the signage.

Neon accented lattice arches and mosaic patterns, also adapted from Mayan stonework found in nearby archaeological sites, are used in the departmental signs for the Deli, the Bakery, Cafeteria and Customer Services. In addition, the decor package also included multi-dimensional, lifelike, hand painted and carved artwork.

For the local shoppers, this is a warm, comfortable and friendly place to shop. It reflects their surroundings, their culture and their heritage.

The individual price cards are fitted into the slots over the tiered merchandise display. The same deep but toned down rose/red color is used and it recalls the departmental signage above.

The grocery area of Super Maz with the specialty shops seen way in the back.

The checkout. Teal and coral appear here along with a big thank you to the departing customers.

SAFEWAY

Broadway, Seattle, WA

Mithun Partners of Seattle, WA, focused on a fresh and energetic look for the Broadway Safeway store. They reflected its "vibrant and highly visible" Capitol Hill location. The store's new exterior and interior design and layout are reoriented not only to address the existing parking area but also to capture the sidewalk and pedestrian traffic. This was achieved with new storefronts and an entry direct from the main pedestrian corridor of the neighborhood—off Broadway. The outdoor seating and the bright neon signage also helped.

"The newly renovated, 23,000 sq. ft. Safeway store creates an expression of the unique identity, history and rich diversity of this older, inner city, neighborhood." The designers/architects went beyond tradition to "provide a fresh expression of historical forms—including graphics, lighting and stylized signage concepts" for this store. The new, vertical art deco format of the Safeway signature is a gentle reminder of the company's 70-year presence and history in this neighborhood.

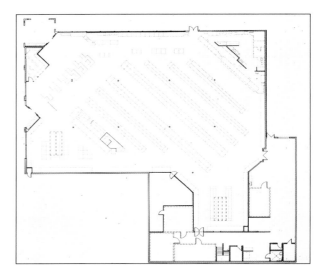

The facade with the neon signage aglow, the vetical format of the art decor Safeway sign adds a vintage touch to the store's facade.

Produce. Waving canopies of green and white striped canvas hang over the island displays of fruits and vegetables. Multi-colored ribbon streamers are suspended down from the skylight that provides daylight to this area.

DESIGN:
Mithun Partners, Seattle, WA

ARCHITECTS:
Richard Utt, AIA/Ron van der Veen, AIA/Kara Moriarty, AIA

INTERIORS/GRAPHICS:
Steve Schell, Schek Design Group, Mt. Vernon, WA

SIGNAGE & BANNERS:
Christian Soltendieck, Northwest Neon & Signage, Seattle, WA

OWNER'S REPRESENTATIVE:
Mitch Johnson, AIA, Safeway, Inc.

PHOTOGRAPHER:
Marty Orchard, Mithun Partners, Joe Manfredini, Seattle, WA

The overall color scheme of red, green, black and white is accented with bright, sizzling neon departmental signage. Note the mirrored valance reflecting the meat display below.

The same strong color pallete is used on the tile covered perimeter walls, as accents on the neutral splattered floor tiles and to accentuate the metal lamp shade covers used to highlight the merchandise presentation.

A view of the floral shop.

Long runs of exposed fluorescent fixtures run diaginally across the open selling floor. Here, a view of the checkout area.

"The interior is dynamic, warm and visually intense," says the design firm. Each department is presented as a small specialty food shop—typical of the ones that have been historically traditional in this area. Each shop's signage and decor is unique. In the Produce, Dairy and Fresh Seafood sections, there are hand painted "historical murals" accented with neon and dimensional letter signage. For the Bakery, replicas of bicycles create an arch that supports the 3D signage. A 15-degree canted wall with a six ft. mirror strip encircles the store and identifies each department with unusual, mirror faced letters.

"These mirror faces reflect and intensify the color and movement of the busy store."

A cohesive color scheme of blue and green earth tones is highlighted with a continuous thread of rich red/plum and touches of black for depth and contrast. "Both color scheme and design elements work synergistically to create an intense, color-rich, environment in which the shopper enjoys the discovery sense of specialty shops." New skylights and the open market style Produce section add to overall desired effect.

JITNEY JUNGLE PREMIER

Jackson, MS

Few retail establishments can claim to be more American in concept than Jitney Jungle, founded in 1918 and a mainstay supermarket chain in Mississippi. Programmed Products Corp. of Plymouth, MI has taken an existing 58,847 sq. ft. store and in ten months created something really new for the 98 store chain to follow. "Although the flavor is truly American, this remodel and expansion displays high level merchandising concepts and eliminates the class and flair of European-style marketplaces."

Red and white canvas awnings and the red neon outlined letters on the neutral facade suggest a "truly American flavor" along with a hint of something yet to come.

Overhead, the ceiling has been painted black "to achieve a comfort level and intimacy." Slatted wood fixtures add to the old-fashioned, farmers market feeling along with the chalkboards with their handwritten price information and fun graphics.

Green and white striped canvas awnings capped with wood planter boxes spilling over with silk foliage and the colorful supergraphics identify the Produce department.

DESIGN:
Programmed Products Corp., Plymouth, MI
Llew M. Reszka, President

ARCHITECT:
Robert Polk, Robert G. Polk Architects, Jackson, MS

PROJECT MANAGER:
Ron Gaines, C.E. Frazier Construction Co.

ARCHITECT-EXTERIOR:
Larry Singleton

FOR JITNEY JUNGLE PREMIER:
PROJECT MANAGER:
Larry Till

V.P. ENGINEERING:
James P. Riley

DIRECTOR OF ENGINEERING:
Randy Shepard

CEILING SYSTEMS:
Glass Block by Decco-Block
Colored Ceiling Tiles by Celotex

LIGHTING:
Lithonia Specialty Lighting

FIXTURES:
Madix and Southern Stores Fixtures, Bessemer, AL

MILLWORK & CUSTOM FIXTURES:
Southern Stores Fixtures

EXTERIOR SIGNAGE:
Rainbow Signs

CANOPIES:
Utrafab & Sunbrella

The black is especially effective in Frozen Foods where the black finished refrigerated cases are mirrored in the polished, black vinyl floor. The suspended arcade over the area is accentuated with silk foliage hanging down over the classic beige and white architectural element.

The floor is patterned in black, beige and white with diagonals, squares and border designs. Black is also used on the ceilings of the perimeter shops to keep the light and activity focused on the merchandise presentation at eye level.

In the Cheese area the green/white awnings, the flower boxes and the light troughs behind the dentil molding trimmed soffits reappear. Wood veneers are used to face the fixtures and wood display fixtures are also used.

The front end of the store contains a cluster of perishable departments and specialties including produce and floral, cheese, deli, bakery, and a juice bar which is "an island of refrigeration set on a chilling surrounding of illuminated glass block."

The ceiling in this area is painted a deep, dark color "to achieve a comfort level and intimacy" which is more evident here due to the greater variety of merchandise and displays.

The grocery area opens up with a lighter colored ceiling and VCT flooring—here accentuating the perimeter. In frozen foods, an elegant and unusual black vinyl floor provides a striking appearance and is congruous with the black refrigerated cases.

The Fruit & Juice Bar is defined by the green canopy structure hanging over it and the illuminated glass block case which shimmers like a giant block of ice. Next to it is the Salad Bar where the color scheme is teal, beige and natural wood. The sign overhead combines teal and coral—like the minitiles set in the white floor.

Pastries & Cakes.

One of several specialty food areas in the Food Court. Each food specialty has its own sign, its own look and identity. All together they create an exciting and colorful area in the supermarket.

The floor design and motif is similar to those in the perishables departments where the tile is ceramic mosaic.

Walls throughout are soft, pastel, neutral tones. The contours of the space are accentuated by architectural treatments such as a highly detailed dentil crown wall wash, and a continuous cove planter box. All the available niches are used for merchandise presentation. "The variety is abounding and the decor and signing is overwhelming with style." The signage, throughout, is a variation on the same style: bold in shape, heavily textured and full of color.

Vertically striped canvas awnings with exposed contrasting frames are mounted to the architectural drops over some of the service departments. Corrugated metals, sweeping arch forms, drop shadow effects and attention to fine trim detail are evident all over the store. Chalkboards are placed over displays for price information. The colorful hand lettering and artistic graphics contrast with the display

Floral. Salmon pink and teal, combined with black and white, predominate in this area.

The same color scheme continues in the Pharmacy.

and decor materials. They "present a playfulness intended to make the shopping experience pleasant and fun."

In addition, there is a full service pharmacy and a video department. At the checkout there is a false, luminous ceiling system to "gradually prepare the shopper for the hot Mississippi sun—and where one can reflect on a positive and truly Premier shopping experience."

The Cafe in the Food Court.

Under a dramatically angled, false illuminated ceiling, the checkout counters are easily located. Each one is identified by its teal and coral number. The bright ceiling device prepares the customer for his/her exit into the hot Mississippi sunshine.

The Fruit & Vegetable area is clean, bright and light. White floors, white fixtures and white walls fin-ished with decorative bands of white tiles are accented with moldings and touches of black. The dropped ceiling has recessed fluorescent fixtures which spread a clear overall light on the produce. Blue/white/yellow pricing signs highlighted with red create a colorful horizontal band under the fascia.

SUPERAMA

Mexico City, Mexico

Superama is the smallest format in the Cifra family of food retail chains. It is more of a "neighborhood" market than the others and thus draws its customers from the immediate area. Superama is positioned as a "stand alone, alternative food store for moderate to upper income families" who regard quality, freshness and service as integral parts of the value quotient.

To satisfy the "stand alone" requirement, the design team of Schafer Associates felt a "strong visual differential" was critical for the 20,000 sq. ft. store. This they could effect with a color system, a level of amenity and a clear statement of policies, values and services. As an "alternative" to the larger scale supermarkets, the Superama position could be accomplished by simplifying the shopping, emphasizing cooking in place of product or category dominance, showcasing a high-quality, theatrical presentation of food and stressing shopping as a personal rather than institutional experience.

Another aspect considered to reinforce the demographics of the shoppers was to make more upscale references: emphasis on a pre-prepared Deli section, easy and efficient shopping and a sense that Superama is "your store" and represents the shopper's lifestyle.

DESIGN:
Schafer Associates, Oakbrook Terrace, IL

The "Salchichoneria" is distinguished by the yellow and blue, neon trimmed, signage on the soffit out front. The wall and fixture scheme is the same here as it was in Produce. Here the price cards make a striped design over the shelved merchandise.

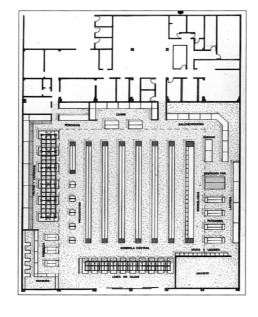

The design firm stressed the concept of "freshness" by positioning the Bakery, Produce, Fish and Meat areas prominently and also making sure that prep areas and sampling areas were visible throughout the store. Visual merchandising and display techniques were used that made "quality" seem within easy reach. This was all further enhanced by the colors and materials used, the attention given to details and the clearly defined signage system.

"Service" is evidenced everywhere. The open, easy-to-shop plan with views of cooking, baking and preparation areas and the strong displays that show-case the selection of wines, the accessible customer service counters and especially the high-speed check-outs, all make shopping Superama a satisfying "personal" shopping experience.

A massive dubonnet colored ceiling grid, made of wood, is suspended over the sleek check-out counters which are finished in the same deep, rich red color. Hanging metal halide lamps and long fluorescent fixtures are combined to affect the ambient light.

CASA LEY

Hermosillo, Mexico

This is the second prototype design created for the Casa Ley hypermarkets by King Design International. This 120,000 sq. ft. mega space is located in Hermosillo, Mexico. The design objective presented to the design firm by the chairman and CEO of the hypermarket chain, Sr. Juan Manuel Ley, was "to create a festive atmosphere—one that was dynamic and yet gave the customer the 'megastore' feeling."

The colors, patterns and motifs used inside the store are all presented out front—on the facade. Red/white/blue and green make a strong statement when seen from the road.

The Dairy area features lavenders, blues, and greens sparkled with red and yellow. The actual roof of the building, seen here, has been painted white with a dark blue band at the curtain wall junction with the ceiling.

The Produce area. The store's owner wanted "a festive atmosphere" and there is a carnival going on in this open, color-filled store. Natural wood box bases support the display of fresh produce under an array of white space frames that, in turn, support the incandescent spots on the attached tracks.

The Sweets area. The floor is a helter-skelter arrangement of various blues, reds, beige and white tiles with the signage still predominantly in cool blue/lavender/gray green which is also seen along the perimeter walls. The arched space frame supports the signage and the banner trim.

DESIGN:
King Design International, Eugene, OR

MARKETING & DESIGN TEAM:
Nancy Wade/Christopher Studach/
Michael Hopper/Jennifer Dean

ARCHITECT:
Coso SA de CV

PHOTOGRAPHER:
Don Winston, Winston Studios, AZ

The carnival feeling is also seen on the floor in the non-food area. Notice the wall treatment behind and how the red headers unify the gondolas.

To accomplish the directive, vibrant colors were used along with "oversized" wall copy, departmental hanging features and banner style signs throughout the market. The green metal grid structures floating overhead "give a light, airy feeling to several departments—eliminating the crowded appearance that can occur with the amount of merchandise offered in Casa Ley stores."

To add even more excitement and dazzle, the design team added even more color and pattern on the lower walls and flooring. Wherever possible the "Ley" logo was incorporated "to help unify the design and promote the local name." To provide a modicum of warmth and comfort in this food fiesta ambience, there is a cafe, up front, with seating where shoppers can take a relaxing or stimulating coffee break.

The use of signage, the merchandise display and the happy, fanciful and carnival color palette have all been enthusiastically endorsed by the Casa Ley shoppers. Together these decorative elements have taken the stress and anxiety out of shopping such a vast space.

Perfumery. The arched space frame overhead delineates the "shop" set amidst the vari-colored tiled floor.

The checkout area is long and impressive with a space frame running the length of it. Several white wire arches interrupt the long run. Red/white/blue are the predominant colors up here and the floor design is simplified to red tiles evenly spaced amid the white tiles.

RANDALL'S

Lexington, KY

This full-service Randall's Supermarket opened in a 47,000 sq. ft. space in the north side of Lexington, KY. What made this project so challenging to the designers was that the supermarket is ringed by at least five other supermarkets including a Winn-Dixie and two Krogers.

One thing that distinguishes this market is that it also includes a pharmacy, a flower shop, a smoke house and a popular and inviting espresso bar. "Randall's is a state-of-the-art, one-stop, supermarket furnishing its patrons with unique services new to this north side community."

The old to introduce the new. Randall's logo, laid in mosaic on the floor, is the shopper's first visual impression of the store. The "Old Paris Pike Market" is a reference to the past—and to the nostalgia that plays such an important part in the store's design.

Part of what makes Randall's a "one-stop supermarket" is the Flower Shop shown here, and the Pharmacy. The black, green and white color scheme is especially effective with the brightly colored flowers.

Splashes of red neon set off the mostly black and white departmental signage. Teal and aqua are the important accent colors here.

DESIGN:
Design Fabrications, Inc., Troy, MI

Produce: The ceiling has been painted a dark color and the metal halide lamps light up the pale gray tile floor, the white and black cases and the natural wood and black trimmed produce display fixtures. Here the designers introduced "a farmer's market"—set out in an open space.

To make the store more memorable and also to set it apart from the competition, the design firm, DFI, created a warm and friendly nostalgic atmosphere by using a pleasant, neutral palette of colors and materials accented with local geographic and historical photos—which set the theme for the store.

Upon entering, the shopper's first visual impression is the Randall's logo laid in mosaic on the floor. The smell and hissing sounds emanating from the espresso bar located to the left of the entrance draw the shopper into an old fashioned "soda fountain" setting which is updated with clear, contemporary colors.

Opposite the Produce department, the specialty shops along the perimeter wall are finished in white tile trimmed with black tile in a checkered pattern. The gray floor in this area is bordered with an intricate geometric tile design in gray, black and white—directly in front of the white cases. Explanatory graphics in black diamond shaped frames, attached at right angles off the soffit, show pictorially what is available in the enclosed cases below.

To emphasize the past, in the Deli department, there is a curved aluminum structure with brass faced lettering reading "Old Paris Pike Market" attached. Behind it—on the wall—is a giant sepia toned photomural of that old local market.

One of the fun highlights of the store is the giant swordfish that appears to be bursting out of the wall signage in the Seafoods department.

The deep, dark green and white color feeling continues up to the checkout where Randall's logo banners identify the check-out lines. Long bands of fluorescent fixtures stretch horizontally across the area to provide bright ambient light.

A cool, illuminated ceiling along with metal halide lamps adds the proper brittle feeling to the Frozen Foods area. The white and blue color scheme completes the chilling process.

To the right of the entrance is the Produce area where the designers carried through the "nostalgia" theme with a "farmers" market set out in the open and airy space. Adding to the excitement and drama of the store, the Seafood shop is highlighted by a giant replica of a swordfish—"exploding from the wall."

Throughout the supermarket, the past is brought up into the present. Over the Deli section is a curved aluminum structure with brass faced letters reading "Old Paris Pike Market" and behind is a mural-sized historical photo of that old local market. In addition to the many historical photos and vintage touches to enhance the "nostalgic atmosphere and home-town feeling," local street names are used on the aisle destination points in the store.

KESSEL PREMIER

Hollywood Plaza, Flint, MI

The newly-designed facade reflects the "upscale and elegant" decor introduced on the inside. The rich blue-green, beige and sharp red colors which decorate the facade, the signing and the awnings also are part of the interior color palette. The fan window in the pitched roof on top suggests Kessel's new upscaled look.

The original store was completely gutted and the 72,400 sq. ft. space was completely redesigned, repositioned and repatterned by Programmed Products Corp. The design objective was to introduce a new shopping pattern while the decor objective was "to develop a package which created a new total image for this small Flint, MI chain whose core area's concentration is their own city."

The decor was to be upscale and elegant and the use of strong accents and the effective lighting of the merchandise was also part of the directive.

Teal-green, black and white are used prominently along with silk foliage which spills out over the angled awnings. The off-white floors are patterned in teal, beige and black. Wood planking is used in the Produce area for the floor finish.

The ceiling has been painted black to focus the shopper on the merchandise. Solid and striped fabric awnings, angled away from the walls, are combined with strong graphics and mural images.

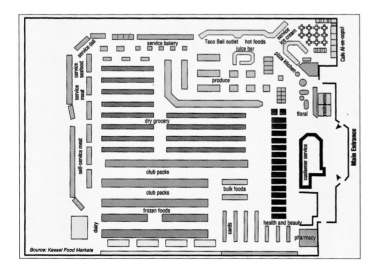

DESIGN:
Programmed Products Corp., Plymouth, MI

PRESIDENT:
Llew M. Reszka

KESSEL'S PROJECT TEAM:
*Tim Kessel, Sr. V.P./Frank Brown,
Facility Development*

ARCHITECT:
Randy Shipman, Grainger Park, Flint, MI

PHOTOGRAPHER:
Llew M. Reszka, PPC

CUSTOM FIXTURES:
RW Displays, Lackawana, NY

LIGHTING:
Lithonia Conyers, GA/Lightoilier, Secaucus, NJ

The seafood shop is distinguished by the bold fish graphic which is illuminated by a pair of reversed billboard lights.

Produce is on the left and Chicken-Meats is in the rear. The Pizza shop is on the right. The awning and foliage motif is consistent throughout.

The Checkout. Under a luminous ceiling surrounded by planters dripping foliage, the green and white checkout counters are lined up. The "today's" color palette is a far cry from the traditional deep burgundy, green and brass colors of yore.

Another view of Produce. In this area the awnings are a solid green and the wood floor contrasts with the shiny white cases that stand on it. Mirrored panels have been applied to the column to make them "disappear."

To accomplish what was required, the PPC design team specified that the perimeter ceiling be painted black since the dark ceiling would focus the shopper on the merchandise displayed below—in the light. The wall surfaces, which are light in color, are wall washed with indirect light—"to provide them with a glow of light." To direct the shoppers through the space, there is high contrast flooring coloration in warm, pastel tones. To add a unique quality to the Produce area, the floor here is covered with a vinyl wood tile.

Striped and solid awnings made of soft, drapable canvas fabric are interspersed throughout the store's layout. They are combined with strong graphics and mural images—angled away from the vertical wall surfaces— "to provide a visual appeal in a very non-traditional way." The lighting plan which brings it all together and creates the "strong contrasts" and com-plements the merchandise, makes use of high-tech lamps and specialty store accent lighting fixtures.

In order to "expand" the space, panels of mirrored glass, six ft. tall, surround the columns that appear on the floor. A food court, up-front, adjacent to the Produce area, includes a Taco Bell, Big Al's Pizza Shop, a Deli, an Ice Cream Counter, rotisserie chicken service and a Cafe Al-ee-oop. Here a shopper can get a complete breakfast (juice, bacon, eggs, toast and coffee) all for 99 cents. In addition to the selected customer services there is a pharmacy and a flower stand—all part of the 60,250 sq. ft. of sales space.

Overall, the color palette is warm and pastel with an accent on trendy teals and muted mauves. According to Llew Reszka, president of PPC, "We've left the colors out in the sun to fade a little." This is quite a contrast from the company's 1980 colors: rich burgundy, deep green and lots of brass.

GRAN BAZAR

Plaza Toluca, Toluca, Mexico

This is a "hypermarket"! Not only is it "Gran"—it is gigantic. The 240,000 sq. ft. space in Plaza Toluca in Toluca is actually large enough to fit four football fields into it. In order to accommodate what is sometimes over one million American dollars in sales a day, there are 2000 carts and a squad of "runners" on roller skates ready to fly through the space getting products or price information. To get the traffic moving, 50 checkout counters are in operation.

The design objective for Schafer Associates for this Gran Bazar centered around organizing this larger-than-life, highly promotional space into a customer-friendly, fun, easy-to-shop environment. To achieve these objectives, the design team combined a simple plan, a strong graphic program and a flexible fixturing system.

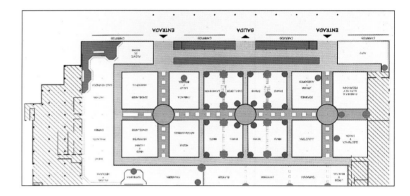

The endless row of checkouts is a first impression indicator as to the size and scope of Gran Bazar. The undulating floor pattern softens the effect of the long, long line of counters.

This larger than life space was turned into a "friendly, fun, easy-to-shop environment" with colorful banners, painted architectural features and graphic details. Black gondolas stand on gray and white splattered tile floors. Floor-to-ceiling columns are painted bright yellow to blend with the many yellow canvas banners. Hanging from the dropped white ceiling grid—along with the banners and signs—are colorful geometric shapes.

Green designates produce and the red grid signs have yellow bands and green lettering. Green is the color for the food area while blue is the color for the general merchandise.

Entering and exiting from the store is made simple and convenient. Two wide entrance openings flank each end of the storefront and a middle door feeds off the enormous centralized bank of checkouts. To further simplify the shopping experience, the space is divided into three worlds of merchandising: food, apparel and general merchandise. A wide, main promotional aisle provides access through the center of the store to each "world" or area.

Promotional focal points and massed out paletted displays of values are featured along these aisles. The promotional aisle intersection in each "world" becomes a reference point and is highlighted by huge overhead circular banners.

The plan strategy is complemented by the graphic system. Each area has its own main color: food/green, apparel/red and general merchandise/blue. Promotional areas throughout are a strong, signature yellow. This color code is consistent from the exterior to the giant wall graphics to the much smaller point of purchase signage.

The giant store banners are red and yellow with the store logo in red/white/blue. The same colors are used in the departmental signs mounted on red grid panels. In this area the gondolas are deep blue and a blue wave motif rolls across the white fascia.

The apparel area is designated the red area as seen by the red lettering on the signs and the red wave sweeping across the perimeter wall. This area is carpeted in a neutral gray and the fixtures here are also gray.

DESIGN:
Schafer Associates, Oakbrook Terrace, IL

PRINCIPALS IN CHARGE:
Robert W. Schafer & Barry Vinyard

DESIGN DIRECTOR:
Dale Wennlund

PROJECT PLANNER/DESIGNER/MANAGER:
Kent Wells

PROJECT GRAPHIC DESIGNER:
Jill Ingrassia

CONSULTANT/ILLUSTRATOR:
Jennifer Wawak

FIXTURE CONTRACTOR:
Lozier

LIGHTING:
Holophone Co., Inc.

PHOTOGRAPHER:
Mauricio Avramow Fotografo, Mexico City, Mexico

In addition to the skylights in the open deck roof of the structure, metal halides provide the clean, open, light feeling. The primary colors appear over and over again since the areas are color keyed for the shoppers' convenience.

The graphics and color concepts for Gran Bazar.

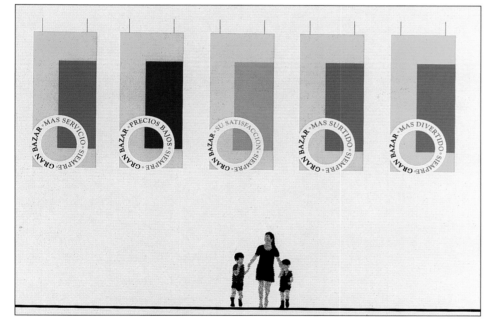

Banners along the promotional aisle boast of the store's guarantees of selection, assortment and savings. Oversized "confetti" shapes and a friendly "wave" motif "bring fun, entertainment and whimsy to the environment."

To complete the design strategy, a flexible fixturing system was adopted. The warehouse fixtures are color coded to the merchandise "world" in which they appear and they allow for massive displays of products below and stocking capabilities above. Each end cap features a display of promotional merchandise.

"Fixtures must be able to change very quickly as products sometimes turn over within a few hours." Presentations are massed out and kept simple and the signage program is integrated with the fixturing for clarity and consistency.

The designers created an authentic, native Mexican ambience. "The bold stripes and saturated colors contribute to a truly Mexican feeling. Departmental signage grids house symbols of related products artistically interpreted from a native Mexican painting style."

The weathered brick facade of Pick 'n Save is trimmed with blue canvas awnings and blue metal trim. The store's logo is in red. The pitched "gables" add interest to the roof silhouette of the store.

EAST POINTE PICK 'N SAVE

Milwaukee, WI

For the design of the East Pointe Pick 'n Save store, the design firm, DFI, was able to incorporate the past into the present. The 32,000 sq. ft. store, located in a revitalized urban area, combines elements of a bygone era with the materials and technologies of today into an exciting marketplace setting. "East Pointe offers the charm of street vendors in a modern day setting as seen through the tall vertical windows located on the outside wall of the Produce department."

In keeping with the "old-new" design concept, DFI specified the use of weathered brick on the exterior of the market. The warm colored bricks are also used as a major interior design element extensively throughout the store. Unfinished corrugated metal canopies are balanced with reproduced murals of European landscapes within the Produce area. Striped duck awnings, mounted on pewter finished metal armatures, are used to identify as well as highlight the Deli department. A merchant seaman and a butcher, supporting a corrugated metal header with neon signage appliqué, flank the Seafood and Meat departments.

The welcome mat is out at Pick 'n Save. The black and white tiles, the old brick and the homey touches of wood are all part of the store's design concept.

Brick walls—like the weathered brick used on the exterior—add to the "old/new" look of this store. Photo blow-ups of European landmarks and landscapes add warmth to the store's design. Unfinished corrugated metal canopies extend out along the perimeter wall over the photomurals and the windows.

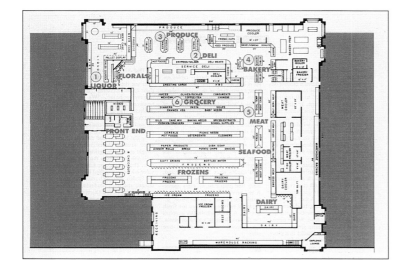

DESIGN:
*Design Fabrications, Inc., Troy, MI
and Steve Royer, Store Planning Mngr., Roundy's, Inc.*

The main attractions of the store are the perimeter perishables departments; the Grocery area has been compacted into a smaller space. "Grocery is designed for volume movement" with limited brands and sizes though the Roundy's private label is featured.

The Meat area combines a service meat case with a 20 ft. long, five tier, self-service case which stocks—as the neon sign affirms—"The Best Meat in Town." Annually, Bob Gold, the store's owner, buys a grand champion prize steer at the state fair plus other "ribbon winners" which are then butchered and sold in the store. Though it may not be a great "profit venture," it does provide good publicity and is good for public relations.

The Deli department is prominently located up front—near the groceries—and it is made available for the quick-lunch trade. People can come in and quickly purchase pizza, hot prepared foods, ethnic delicacies, salads, sandwiches and such. The Deli accounts for 6.5% of the store's sales.

Deli. A dominant black framework of lumber extends out from the wall over the wood and white trimmed black cases in the Deli area. Blue and warm beige striped awnings angle away from the framework revealing the black and white grid panel behind it. The same beige and blue color combination reappears on the rear wall of the shop below where the pale coral color and blue are joined in a decorative band on the white tile wall. A row of spots is lined up along the lower edge of the framework to light up the merchandise displayed in the cases below.

A dimensional butcher flanks the Gold's Market where the seafood is sold. The seaman at the helm is on the far right. The remainder of the area is done in black and white and trimmed with "watery" decorative elements.

Dark blue, natural wood and white take over in the Bakery. A large photomural of baked goods is framed in a crescent shape below the raised Bakery letters.

European details abound in the store interior such as the $18,000 ornate cappuccino machine which was imported from Italy and the mural size photographs of noted European landmarks—to evoke the atmosphere of an open air market. An imported Japanese wood veneer covers the floor of the "power aisle" and it complements the teal and salmon color scheme of the space. The color and materials palette is further enriched with the brick wall treatments, the "pewter" accents, the corrugated metals, striped duck and the natural woods.

The various specialty areas are highlighted, as previously mentioned, with "canopies" and headers as well as decorative signage and checkerboard patterns. On the front wall of the store there are large clocks showing the time in different financial centers around the world. In the foyer there is a wall filled with glazed and fired tiles made by local children stomping barefoot in wet potter's clay. The store's shopping carts are lined up under the decoratively-framed tiles.

The design success of East Pointe Pick 'n Save is shared with Steve Royer, the store planning manager for Roundy's, Inc. and the owners of the market, Bob and Helga Gold.

Up on the front wall—just past the checkout counters and flanked by old brick piers—are clocks showing the time in different financial centers around the world. The old fashioned cast iron black lamp-post holds the checkout line number and adds still another nostalgic touch to the store's look.

HARVEST FRESH PRODUCE

The Produce department in the new prototype design for the Winn-Dixie supermarkets shows the light and attractive new color palette of teal, rose, hot pink, beige and white. Non-slip quarry tiles are used to border the area. The striking pink band is part of the strong, horizontal linear design in the new look.

DESIGN:
CIP International, Fairfield, OH
Thomas Huff, CEO & Creative Director
for Winn-Dixie: Daniel Carhill, AIA, Dir. of Store Design

WINN DIXIE MARKETPLACE

Doverplum S/C, Poinciana, FL

The design objective presented to CIP International for the new Winn Dixie "Marketplace and Food Pavilion" was—"to create a brightly lit, service-oriented supermarket—yet still deliver the company's commitment to being the industry's 'low price leader.'"

Greater emphasis than in the past was to be on the fresh foods and services—building a bigger perishables business—especially with prepared foods, convenience and take-out orders. The design firm took on the challenge to create a store that combined the convenience of one-stop shopping with the fun and excitement of a dynamic food court setting.

The Food Pavilion or food court, takes up more than a fifth of the store's total space. A deep rose/pink band cuts a swath through the space over the cool, blue-green canopies that extend out over the specialty areas. Wall washers, fluorescents, and spots are combined in the store's lighting plan.

Meats & Fish. The rear walls of the service areas are a pale, sand/peach color with an occasional inset of teal and white outlined in black. The free standing floor fixtures have teal colored bases to match the canopies in the area and the accent tiles on the floor.

The Deli Foods area of the Food Pavilion

Baked Foods. The non-slip quarry tiles border the counters. Note how the store's palette is reinforced with the colored napkins used in the baskets which are filled with the baked goods.

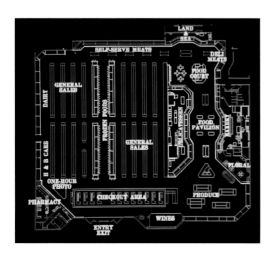

Nearly 20% of the 51,000 sq. ft. of the prototype design is devoted to the up-front food court. The Food Pavilion features enlarged Deli, Hot Foods, Bakery, Fresh Fruit & Melon Bar, Soup & Salad Bar, Service Meat and Seafood areas and a sitdown dining area. There are also many self-service food items as well. The individual "shops" were given their own boundaries by means of simple floor tile patterns which could still be flexible when merchandising requires area to expand or contract. Non-slip quarry tile is used in front of the service cases as well as in other areas where moisture might accumulate and present safety problems.

The sitting area of the Food Pavilion where shoppers can rest, have some coffee or sample any of the many prepared foods available.

Lighting played an important part in upgrading the company's prototype design. Fluorescent lamps on the ceiling and as perimeter wall washers provided an overall, well-lit sales area. Suspended pendant light fixtures were added to enhance the fresh merchandise displayed on island fixtures. The use of energy saving Octron light bulbs and fixtures increased the overall light output without running up energy costs.

The design firm selected up-to-date colors to use on the selling floor "to create a more cheerful atmosphere."

*Other views of the
Food Pavilion and the
Special Shops in it.*

The Flower Shop literally glows with pink, from the almost solid pink tile floor to the pale pink tinted horizontal fascia. The warm incandescent lighting adds to the overall blush.

The Pharmacy.

The Wine Cellar is located near the checkout counters. Prepackaged ice is conveniently located next to it.

The design concept also features three dimensional components, highlighted by linear lines, "which accentuate the expansiveness of the sales area."

The in-store graphics play a vital role in identifying the many services and the all-important "cost saving" theme of Winn Dixie.

With this new format, The Marketplace & Food Pavilion, Winn Dixie meets the challenge of eliminating all of the reasons why shoppers would go to alternative formats. It provides the shopper with more fresh foods, an increased variety of convenience foods — and all in an easy-to-shop and pleasant retail environment.

Checkout. Under a "roof" with a deep rose/pink band on top and pink and teal striping below, the checkout lanes are illuminated by fluorescents in the "roof." Simple horizontal signs indicate the counters below. The four tile checkered pattern used on the floor and on some of the walls in the specialty shops is also decoratively applied to the fascia of the hanging structure.

CHANNEL ISLANDS CO-OP

St. Peter, Jersey, England

The entrance facade into the Channel Islands Co-op.

This store, the largest Co-op on the Islands, has recently been redesigned, renovated, and enlarged by an additional 9000 sq. meters. The new design concentrates on a whole new section of specialty and fresh food departments spread around the perimeter of the store; the delicatessen, bakery, dairy, and fresh produce areas as well as the wines and spirits section. Fitch's design team carried out the principles of strong departmental demarcation and identity and used an unusually bold color scheme to support the product.

The Market within the Market. Fresh produce grown on the Islands is presented in a casual, colorful, and country manner.

A view of the selling floor of the market with bright red columns adding a sense of vitality to what could be a neutral color scheme.

DESIGN:
Fitch, London, England

ARCHITECT/PROJECT MANAGER:
A.S.M., Bristol, England

The Fresh Produce area has a market ambience where the local Jersey products are featured. The foods are displayed on large food bins with prices chalked up on slates. Traditional scales are also used for practical as well as decorative reasons. A ceramic tile wall is used behind to "suggest cleanliness" and the earthy terra cotta flooring also helps to delineate this area from the basic thoroughfare.

The orange tiles in the Bakery area are there to "suggest oven-warmth" and a deep blue is used as an accent behind the freshly-baked breads. Baskets and wood are also employed in the complementary orange and blue scheme. A rail above the counter runs around the perimeter as a multi-functional "flagging" device for products, blackboards, scales, and especially the accent lighting.

The Delicatessen.

The Wine and Spirits department combines wooden wall shelf units with specially-designed wooden gondolas. Note how the bottles are angled forward to make reading the labels easier for the prospective buyer.

As a contrast and complement to the meat products on display in the Fresh Meat area, avocado was selected. It appears in the Delicatessen area as well.

A natural birch backdrop appears in the Wines and Spirits department as a foil for the medium range wines. The more expensive bottles are displayed on individual gondolas with the products angled towards the shopper. The soft, low-keyed lighting provides the desired "wine cellar" ambience. A lectern holds books with information for the interested wine buyer; what wines go with which foods, etc.

Two views of the Bakery area where the orange colored tiles suggest oven warmth and the blue tiles act as a complement for the freshly-baked breads.

The facade of Red Food is white and pale gray with Red Food in bright red. A blue fan window, over the store's entrance, continues as a glazed barrel vault in the store.

RED FOOD STORE

Farragut, TN

Red Food Stores, a chain of about 70 stores, was determined to break away from the popular merchandising format which utilizes the "power alley" concept. Instead of placing the service departments along the perimeter walls, Red Rood Stores, working with the designers at Programmed Products Corp., created a central "staging area." Here, the shopper finds produce, produce prep, deli, bakery, floral and pharmacy. This central stage is surrounded by food shelving to the right and with non-foods and beauty & health products to the left. Meat, dairy and frozen foods are in the rear.

The refrigerated cases, white striped in red, are shown under a series of pitched wood frame "pediments," open and light, but still strong enough in color to identify the area. The color corresponds to the blue supergraphics on the perimeter fascia on the right. A yellow and green circle informs the shopper about the classification of product available here. Incandescent spots in white cannister fixtures, attached to the row of inverted "V"s, provide warm light to the merchandise displayed below.

Part of the centrally-located "staging area" of the new layout is Produce. Floating green wood-frame tent tops bring prominence to the merchandise displayed on the off-white cases on the white floor. The cases are striped in red like the supergraphics on the wall on the left.

DESIGN:
Programmed Products Corp., Plymouth, MI
Llew M. Reszka, President

Yellow = Dairy. There is no missing the bright, butter yellow and white soffit treatment that carries the red "stamp" of Dairy. Wood grain panels, hung at an inclined angle, make a half canopy over the refrigerated cases below.

"This shopping pattern creates the perception of a store within a store and attracts attention to the food presentation." The shopper is returned time and again as she proceeds through the perimeter shelving aisles. Mobile merchandising fixtures are used making it possible to change the product displays to meet any demands. "Through this flexibility, Red Food achieves the key to survival in today's marketplace—changeability."

The store's position as a "super warehouse" is underscored in the 57,000 sq. ft. space by the utilitarian fixturing and the lighting plan which includes metal halides for the ambient, general light. HQI track lighting serves for accent lighting and fluorescents around the perimeter act as the wall washers.

What else but Meat could be represented by Red? This area is dominated by the sharp red in the decor and signage. In this area the seal is green and yellow.

The same decorative signage continues in the non-food areas of the store.

*The green "Deli" over the refrigerated cases is
complemented by the soft rose color that borders
the counters on the floor.*

The prescription drug department.

The multi-colored color scheme was selected for its
"ability to create visual excitement and appetite
appeal." The colors and graphics are used to simulate a "super label" approach to departmental identity. Large graphics appear on multi-colored accent
backgrounds and coordinate with the promotional
and customer service statement banners used in each
department.

The final result is "a super warehouse format which
generates the appeal of constant promotion—literally
a festival of foods."

The decorative signage continues in the check-out area.

The Flower Shop is located out on the floor and it is delineated by the white space frame suspended over it. White spots, attached to the frame, light up the merchandise.

The Bakery is located under the giant red sign and it is surrounded by feature signs. Wood wall fixtures and a rose colored floor serve to mark off this area from the main aisle.

GEANT CASINO

St. Etienne, France

Groupe Casino is the third largest food retailer in France and as it nears its 100th anniversary, it operates 2,500 small stores, 300 superstores and 70 hypermarkets. Hypermarkets have been on the rise in France where land is relatively inexpensive and so structures over 100,000 sq. ft. in size with wide aisles are not rare. Casino is leading the way in introducing "design" and "graphic decor" into the French grocery industry and they contracted Crabtree Hall/Plan Creatif to create the look for future hypermarkets by prototyping the design in the St. Etienne store.

The facade of Geant Casino

The Geant Casino sign as seen from the road.

Green tiles also cover the rear prep walls in the fresh Seafood area and two giant fish tanks, set into illuminated recesses in the back wall, are filled with live crustaceans. Pictures of fish and fishing decorate the wall.

The Produce department has vibrant green tent tops hanging down over the islands of produce displays. Drop lights with green metal shades, within the tent tops, provide the accent light for the produce. The floor fixtures are made of wood and they are trimmed with dark green. White ceramic tiles are laid on the floor and some of the walls are covered with smaller dark green tiles.

For this hypermarket everything was redesigned—not only the store but the small mall attached to it with its 35 retail stores and three restaurants. The design firm worked on every aspect of the development from architecture, interior design, graphics, signage, car park layout—even to the staff uniforms.

A continuous rooflight was introduced which runs the length of the mall. "This offers maximum natural light and allows the front of the hypermarket building itself to be washed with light from the mall at night." The volume of the space, over 110,000 sq. ft., was broken up into strongly differentiated areas, "to stimulate the customer's shopping experience while retaining the clarity of the hypermarket fixture layout and circulations." This was accomplished through varying the ceiling heights, lighting intensities and the finishes applied.

Up near the entrance into this hypermarket is a 1,500 sq. meter department that contains a wide selection of "white goods": ranges, refrigerators, washers, etc. A sweeping, undulating ceiling furnished with incandescent spots hangs over this area.

With 18,000 items, Food represents 53% of the store's turnover. The specialized fresh food areas include a hot pizza corner, a delicatessen and cheese area, and a fresh fish department which is enhanced by two large tanks behind the counter filled with live crustaceans. The Wine department is subdivided by the wine growing areas and stars a central display of vintage clarets in their wooden cases.

The shopper enters through a 1,500 sq. meter audio and electrical department which has a wide selection of white goods (ranges, washers, dryers, refrigerators, freezers) plus a wall with a display of over 100 TV sets. Other non-food departments include a book

shop, a fashion and shoe department and a large health and beauty section. "The result is a contemporary, inviting and effective store environment."

Since personal service is an important part of French food shopping, the master butchers, bakers and fishmongers are all specially costumed "to further enhance the professionalism of the group."

Rather than the old-time system where each store was responsible for its own graphics and signage, Crabtree Hall/Plan Creatif has devised a flexible point of sale system "whereby the individualism of the graphics can be retained within the new tightly controlled signage system."

*The Frozen Foods department is cool and light. Yellow metal shades cover the metal halide
lamps that are suspended over the white refrigerated cases which are trimmed with yellow.
Yellow and red promotional signage keeps the look consistent. In the ceiling, metal halides as
well as the skylights provide the general light for the store.*

*A view of the mall that is attached to Geant Casino. A continuous glazed
roof runs the length of the mall and offers maximum natural light.*

DESIGN:
Crabtree Hall/Plan Creatif,
London, England

PARTNER IN CHARGE:
Gerard Lecoeur

PHOTOGRAPHER:
Robert Gregoire

REAY'S RANCH MARKET

Scottsdale, AZ

King Design International of Eugene, OR has worked with Gordon Reay on several other interior design projects, but this one called for the remodeling of a vacant 17,000 sq. ft. store in a Scottsdale mall. "Gordon wanted a store that was compatible with this area—and the interior must reflect the 'upscale' and 'exclusive' feeling, while keeping the natural foods store's appeal." The client also required that certain signature elements that have appeared in the Reay's Ranch Market in Tuscon be included in this design as well.

DESIGN:
King Design International, Eugene, OR

MARKETING & DESIGN TEAM:
Nancy Wade/ChristopherStudach/
David Thigpen

PHOTOGRAPHER:
Don Winston, Winston Studios, AZ

The colors of Reay's Ranch are soft and gentle: warm beige, a teal and light natural woods. Here, at the checkout, one can see the neutral palette in use with the skeletal roof overhead from which the pendant lamps are hung.

The produce area. A superstructure of natural wood accentuates this part of the store as does the diagonally laid white tile floor patterned in deep sand color with a border of the same tiles surrounding the space. The perimeter wall is a pale, teal with dark green and copper dimensional letters applied over it. Wooden bushels add to the marketplace ambience and they also serve as decorative containers/displayers for some of the products. The area glows with the warm light emanating from the spots attached to the overhead wood structure.

Seafood is on the right. The fascia is highlighted with bands of a deeper green and neon signage. Opposite are the bulk foods bins where natural wood fixtures dominate. At the far end—beyond the wood "roof"—is produce.

The same soft teal appears in a checkered pattern with off-white on the floor. The wall behind the specialty shop is covered in several shapes of green ceramic tiles laid on the diagonal, to create the diamond shaped border design under the wood framed soffit. White neon signage is set off the white surface and separated by the framed teal and pale yellow diamond shapes.

The floral shop.

Bakery and Deli.

Several things were of great importance to the over-all look of the space and probably most critical was the placement of the curtain walls—and, of course, the specialty lighting. The color and materials palette was adapted from the one originally created for the Tucson store: natural light woods, white, teal, and dark green. Since this new space was smaller, the graphics had to be scaled down to be compatible with the space and windows were "simulated"—to open up the space. To further enhance the "open, airy feel-ing," the designers added planters filled with silk plants and to add to the "Southwest" ambience that was desired, wooden beams were incorporated into the design. They also serve to emphasize certain areas and departments in the market.

A special consideration was the sit-down cafe which became part of the total market design. Here, vinyl wood strip flooring was used to create a more com-fortable and homey feeling for the shoppers. An out-of-doors eating area — under a giant canopy—was also added to accommodate additional seating. VCT flooring was used in assorted patterns to tile the rest of the store with a special change made in the pro-duce section.

The designers added accents of neon — "sparsely used" in the Seafood, Deli, Bakery and Coffee areas. This provided the "extra sparkle" requested by the client. Overall the store has "a classic elegant feeling which fits in well with the area and the expectations of the customers."

FOOD GIANT

London, England

Food Giant is a new concept for Gateway Food Markets. It is a discount operation and this giant warehouse setting (82,000 sq. ft. with 51,000 sq. ft. devoted to sales) was designed by Crabtree Hall/Plan Cratif. It was designed with a distinctive trading image "aimed to change customers' perception of discount shopping—making it a respectable and fun alternative to more mainstream supermarkets."

Everything about Food Giant is colorful—and fun. There is a strong American influence here: piped-in '50s and '60s music, pop-art details, strong bright primary colors and even the outfits worn by the staff. The official costume consists of red and yellow

DESIGN:
Crabtree Hall/Plan Creatif, London, England

PARTNER IN CHARGE:
David S. Mackay

PHOTOGRAPHER:
Jon O'Brien

The giant warehouse type market is alive with American-style graphics of the '60s: brilliant colors, day-glo, patterns clashing with patterns and "pop," "wow" and "wham" signs. Here is the checkout area with a supergraphic mural above it and a wildly checkerboarded wall beside it.

Day-glo, fluorescent colors jump out from the acid green and polka dotted walls. The H.V.A.C. systems overhead visibly travel through the store painted in strong colors that contrast with the bright blue ceiling.

sweat shirts trimmed with green, yellow and white Food Giant logo. There is nothing timid or subtle about the fluorescent messages and the sharp colors on the advertising posters that fill the sales space.

The central aisle—as one enters the store—is the "power aisle" and it gets special attention. Around the store's perimeter, generous secondary aisles encourage shoppers to browse in the fresh food sections which account for 40% of the total sales space. The Food Giant has its own in-store bakery, patisserie and fish departments as well as a centrally-located produce market. The Giant Cafe, fashioned after an American period diner, serves snacks and light repasts all day long.

This market, one of the largest food halls in London, has 37 checkout stations and offers 10,000 fresh food and grocery items in the warehouse style environment. The store is illuminated by economical to maintain high, bay, discharge lighting.

"Everything about Food Giant is colorful and fun!" Graphics and signage are full of snap, crackle and pop-art—vitalized with strong primary colors and cartoon exaggeration.

All the price signs have an impromptu feeling about them—as though they were just scrawled off. Long rows of fluorescent fixtures line up over the selling floor.

The gondolas are finished in school bus yellow for high visibility and the speckled white tiled floors help reflect the light from the metal halides hung over the "power aisle" of the store.

Service is a very important part of Food Giant's image and that includes a helpful staff which will assist the shopper in getting the shopping bags out to the parked cars.

One of the really unique service amenities is Giant Club. Here parents can leave their children to play in a supervised area while they shop. The "play pen" area is complete with "diddy toilets" and everything in the play area—the slides, the "walls," the furniture—are all made of PVC giant reproductions of food packages. These "packs" are sponsored by the major food manufacturers who see their logo-ed packages used as toys for the children. Everything is "padded"—"a child's dream"—"they can throw themselves around to their hearts' content."

According to Paul Jackson, general manager of the store, "Food Giant is alive! Everybody's singing and there's no aggression. The atmosphere dissipates it. Food Giant is not cold, sterile, clinical and impersonal; it is a shopping experience."

The checkout area. The final and total blast of color and fancy makes this "a fun alternative to more mainstream marketplaces." There is little that is "mainstream" here.

The warm, buff colored floor is neutral, utilitarian and easy to keep clean. The mobile fixtures and casual wood display units add to a "marketplace" ambience in the Produce section of the store which is located up front for greatest impact.

The new 79,000 sq. ft. flag-ship store as seen at night when the signage glows in the dark. A separate, signed entrance leads to the Market Place Cafe.

BAKER'S

Eagle Run, Omaha, NE

Growing with the city of Omaha, the very successful Baker's Foods came to Peterson Associates in search of a new retail image which could be applied to their future stores as well. For this 79,000 sq. ft. flagship store, the designers came up with a new credo—their forecast for future food retailing. It is, "Tune down decor and tune up merchandise presentation."

The strategy was to reinforce Baker's commitment to quality, freshness, and value while creating an open and animated food store/marketplace. The approach, adopted by the design firm, was to avoid self-conscious decor and superfluous details that tend to communicate "high costs" to customers. "The store is to be an honest and straightforward value driven approach to food merchandising where the product is truly the star."

Some of the customer service desks are lined up along the wall opposite Produce. The blacked out structural ceiling is spotted with HID fixtures.

In the Bakery the customer is able to watch the freshly baked foods come out of the very visible ovens lined up along the white tiled walls.

The customer enters into a super-sized entrance vestibule with full height windows that give the shopper a panoramic view of the total store. A painted waterline and lighting height at 16 ft. demarcate the ceiling from the production areas. "The effect carries your eye to the display level and features the activity of preparing food." The floor, a warm buff color that goes with the fixtures and the merchandise presentation, is utilitarian and easy to keep clean. Mobile fixtures and casual display vignettes in natural wood also convey the "marketplace" feeling.

The ambient lighting comes from the HID fixtures while spotlights showcase much of the perishables and signature products. The image-building Produce department is strategically positioned at the front entrance for greatest impact.

The Deli department.

Also in the Bakery, the chalkboards attached to the soffit supply up-to-the-minute information on what is available and what it costs. The informality of this signage complements the store's image.

The same neutral color feeling continues in Fresh Seafood and Meat. The painted water line and the lighting height at 16 ft. demarcate the ceiling from the production areas.

Groceries are lined up on white gondolas under the suspended HID lamps. The simple, clear aisle markers make it easier for the shoppers to find what they are looking for. The store's design indicates "an honest and straight-forward value driven approach to food merchandising."

Special feature areas are located beneath the strong yellow banners that are readily visible on the vast selling floor.

Floral, Housewares, Specials and Fish follow Produce within an open plan that "allows customers to mingle with the production associates so conversation can flow easily back and forth." Identification graphics and separate icons that relate to specific categories are used to express the individual personalities of the signature categories. "Thus, the personality of the store materializes through the collective impression of all the categories graphics."

As in other Barker's supermarkets, this one features a sit-down restaurant. It represents a "backyard" or "patio" atmosphere—perfect for casual family dining. Clapboard siding, window awnings and overhead trellises capture the out-of-doors ambience.

The Video store. One of the customer service stands and counters located near the front of the store.

The Flower market is another service-oriented shop. "The identifying graphics and separate icons that relate to specific categories are used to express the individual personalities of the signature categories."

The Kitchen Court carries an array of kitchen and household accessories.

DESIGN:
Peterson Associates, Hinsdale, IL

PROJECT PRINCIPAL:
David Sellke

GRAPHIC DESIGNER:
Stephanie Arakawa Moore

COLOR/MATERIAL DESIGN:
Stefanie Anderson

PROJECT ARCHITECT:
Savage, Findley, Palandri & Ling

GENERAL CONTRACTOR:
Vrana & Sons Construction Co.

CUSTOM CASEGOODS:
Designer Wood

LIGHTING:
Lithonia and Lightlab

GROCERY FIXTURES:
Lozier

The Wine department is set out on the floor but identified by a special hanging sign.

Red, black and gray are
combined to highlight
the checkout lanes with
each suspended sign
band carrying its own
fluorescent lighting.

The facade of the new Despar store in Albaville in Italy. The oversized buff colored brick facade is decorated with a bold fascia of vibrant red that carries the supermarket name. An arced glass canopy welcomes the shoppers in front the parking lot.

DESPAR

Albavilla, Italy

This Despar operation is typical of the supermarket stores located throughout Italy. Located in the suburbs—but close to built-up communities, the stores usually average 150,000 - 200,000 sq. ft. in size and are situated to "fully exploit the potential market." Usually the fresh/perishables departments comprises at least 50% of the total selling space.

The Despar supermarket attempts in its design and layout to approximate "your neighborhood supermarket"—but on a much larger scale. The character and atmosphere of the store is underlined by "flying architectural structures"—by the use of different colors and by the special lighting effects used to highlight the various merchandise categories. To empha-

Dark wood, black and brass accents plus an arcade of half arches turn the prepared foods area into an elegant Euro-style, gourmet shop in the midst of the supermarket setting. Incandescent lights also contribute to the upscaled look of this shop.

Produce. Angled wood fixtures present the fresh fruits and vegetables for tiered viewing. They look as though they were still in their original wood crates. The buff colored ceramic tile floor is neutral and the linear fluorescent fixtures hang over the island displays. Artificial flowers cascade off the light fixtures—adding a garden and outdoors atmosphere to the Produce area.

DESIGN:
Despar's Store Design/Planning Department
Marco Orsenigo, Director

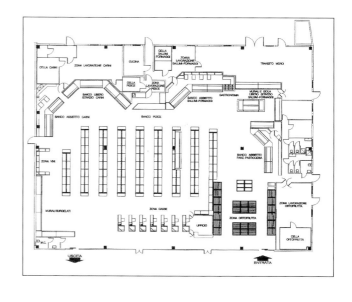

Set beneath a red tiled roof/canopy is the Butcher shop and Meat area. Natural wood bases support the refrigerated cases and a border of wood planks runs the length of the shop over the ceramic tiled rear wall. A window permits the shopper to look into the freezer.

The same feeling is continued in the Deli area at Despar.

Freshly made pizza—to order—is also available. The red brick faced ovens are behind the counter and the pizza maker works in full view of the shoppers on the aisle. Chalk boards indicate the specials and the prices. Incandescent spots are used to illuminate this shop.

size Despar's position as a "quality supermarket," great stress is placed on promoting the concept of product freshness and the vast selection available to the shopper.

This store is almost 125,000 sq. ft. in size with almost 80,000 sq. ft. devoted to sales. A large area is devoted to parking. After the generous allotment of space for grocery shelving, the largest amount of selling space is given to fresh produce—fruits and vegetables—followed closely by the dairy section. Frozen foods are prominently set out in the Albaville store followed in descending order by: delicatessen (salumi, formaggi, gastronomia), self service meat, butchered meat, bakery and fish.

As anticipated by the space allocations, the grocery section accounts for about 36% of the total sales followed by the meat area (14.5%), the delicatessen (13.2%), and the dairy (12.39%). Non-food products only account for 2.28% of the total sales.

Natural wood fixtures accented with red are used for the wine storage. A neon sign announces the presence of the wine shop in the market.

DESIGN:
King Design International, Eugene, OR

MARKETING & DESIGN TEAM:
Nancy Wade/Christopher Studach/
Michael Hopper

ARCHITECT:
Nadel Partnership

LIGHTING:
Taylor Electric, Portland, OR

PHOTOGRAPHER:
Gary Silk, Los Angeles, CA

GELSON'S

Encino, CA

Gelson's is known in Southern California as "the dominant upscale grocer" of the area and King Design International looked forward to providing the exterior and interior design for this 21,000 sq. ft. Encino store. In order to provide the right look and ambience, the design team studied the surrounding area and the clientele to "ensure that this particular store enhanced rather than detracted from this area." Although the store does draw from all parts of the San Fernando Valley, the majority of Gelson's shoppers are from an established and affluent group.

Along with the mainstays of the market—the Produce, Meat and Dairy areas—the designers were called upon to integrate floral and gift baskets, wine, chocolates, bakery, deli, sushi and a coffee bar. In addition, a housewares section was also added. In order to accomplish all this successfully, lighting became a key element in the overall design plan.

The smart and stylish facade of Gelson's Encino store is red brick and accented with white framework, rounded awnings and a glassed, greenhouse-type entry area—for the comfort of the incoming or exiting customers.

Gelson's look is introduced in Produce. The store was designed to appeal to the established and affluent shopper. Hanging "alabaster" pendant fixtures provide most of the light here along with wall washers and some accent lighting in the Cookery & Gifts Department along the back wall.

To the other side of Produce is the Bakery. Wood valences of pecan walnut color bands help to distinguish this supermarket as well as unify the assorted individual service areas in it.

The same, warm sophisticated palette continues into Fresh Meats and Seafood. Tiled walls are embellished with geometric patterns in colors used throughout the store. The MR16 lamps add brightness and sparkle to the merchandise on display. Note the greenery over the tiered meat case on the left.

Foliage is used as an accent and as an overall element in the store's decor. Green plants fill the planter box valence in Cheese. The lighting for the wall and refrigerated cases is contained within the base of the "planter boxes."

A walnut and pecan trimmed gondola— out on the floor— serves as the Floral Shop.

With the help of Taylor Electric of Portland, OR, King Design International developed a complete lighting plan which "created light filled aisles and dramatic highlighting of merchandise." In addition, the use of hanging "alabaster" pendant fixtures and the sconces in the service sections all contributed to the "elegance" of the market setting. In keeping with the upscaled attitude, the color scheme is neutral but not dull; two shades of wood were used and complemented with moss green, beige and copper. The chalk white walls set these colors and materials off to their best advantage.

King Design International was also responsible for the exterior graphics. The original "sit-down" area in the main entrance was next to the parking lot, so now a glassed-in area is provided for Gelson's customers who are waiting for their cars or to load up. This is part of two new entrance designs which have been dramatized with strong architectural features and new lighting systems.

"We gave them a comfortable, well lighted, flower filled area in which to sample Gelson's fine foods."

The graphics and detail elements used in the Gelson's store design.

MY CITY FOOD MARKET

Shinjuku, Tokyo, Japan

My City is a 480,000 sq. ft. vertical shopping center located in Tokyo's Shinjuku section. The ten-level complex is built over one of Tokyo's largest rail stations. Located below ground level is the great food market which connects with the city's subway system and thus offers commuters a multitude of choices for eating and food shopping.

The green market/food court/take-out shops and restaurants also cater to the hundreds of thousands of office workers in this highly populated part of Tokyo. The market demographics of this area have changed since the structure originally went up. The "new wave of young, middle-income workers" now in the Shinjuku section have more upscaled tastes. My City was also pressured to change—and change drastically—because of what has happened in updating in the department stores around it.

Visual Japan, the architect selected by Shinjuku Station to bring about this "change," recommended that FRCH (then known as SDI/HTI) be brought in for the designing. Visual Japan and FRCH have worked on many Japanese projects in the past. Koji

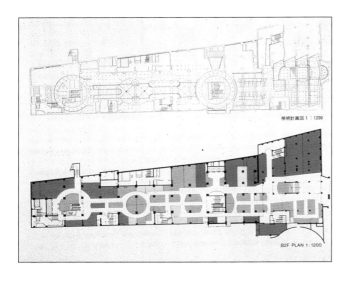

DESIGN:
*FRCH Design Worldwide (formerly SDI/HTI),
New York, NY*

*My City is a newly renovated
and redesigned vertical mall
located over the Shinjuku
Station in Tokyo. The food
court/market is located below
street level—as is traditional
in most Japanese stores.*

Commuters racing to and from the busy subway station can find a quick snack—convenient shopping—or even time out in the My City food area. This marble and granite hallway, below street level, is illuminated by pyramid-shaped skylights that become part of the plaza design at street level.

Ido, director of Visual Japan, in an interview with a Japanese design publication said, "American designers are free from fixed and rigid ideas about interior design. Not only do they have splendid skills in composing space, coordinating colors and materials and using environmental lighting and architecture to form a harmonious whole, they also express their ideas in dynamic ways that Japanese wouldn't attempt."

As in the fashion levels, the food area has wide aisles and good circulation paths. The terrazzo floors are decorated with large scale patterns in neutral contrasting colors. The lighting combines incandescent spots with ceiling washing fluorescent strips.

Curves, arcs and sweeping lines are added to the overall design of My City. It is "an icon for My City" — "it reinforces the mall's identity and serves as a unifying element for all floors."

The American design team planned a three part strategy for changing the look, texture and identity of the total mall and the food area in the lower level which is typical of markets found in department stores.

To bring natural light into My City's two below-ground levels, the lowest level being the food area, FRCH created pyramid-shaped skylights which also serve as focal points on the outdoor plaza. As in the fashion levels above, every effort was made to create a greater feeling of spaciousness. Wider circulation aisles were designed and dramatic geometric ceiling patterns were also added. The built-in lighting in the ceilings makes them appear higher than they are since here the ceiling height is only about nine feet. "The ceiling designs also add visual interest and direct traffic flow."

The more logical circulation system encourages traffic flow throughout each floor. Terrazzo floors with large scale patterns in contrasting but neutral colors also help to define the areas and the "shops" located in each area. The circular form—"an icon for My City"—was introduced at each entrance, point of circulation and in the dropped ceiling designs. The curved forms "reinforce the mall's identity and serve as a unifying element for all the floors."

A newly-designed logo and specially created graphics and signage also added to the new look of My City. "The bright, open feeling and dynamic design have given My City an exciting new identity which particularly appeals to Tokyo's growing ranks of younger consumers."

Though the ceilings are low (only about nine ft.), the built-in lighting makes them seem higher than they are. "The ceiling design also adds visual interest and directs traffic flow."

A typical food vendor area.

One of the small dining areas in My City. Note how the curves and sweeping lines are introduced into the design of the area and how they are reinforced in the ceiling pattern and by the detailing of the terrazzo floors.

WINN DIXIE

Westland Promenade S/C, Hialeah, FL

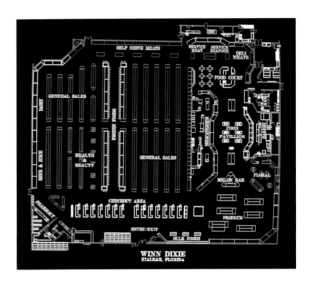

For the Winn Dixie store in Hialeah, Thomas Huff and the creative team at CIP International took their inspiration for the store's decorative theme from the Caribbean. "This store features the palette of colors and shades as seen through the eyes of Caribbean people: white for the beach, green for the coconut palms, and the brilliant colors of the island flowers." This design features sharp, lively colors and is quite different from the look of the Winn Dixie store in Poinciana designed by the same design firm and previously presented in this book.

The designers used an "up-to-date" palette to create a more cheerful selling atmosphere. Up at the checkout area we are introduced to the soft, muted palette of nature-inspired colors sparked with the excitement of the Caribbean: soft greens, grayed blues, muted corals, sand and white. A pale blue border is used to border the sand beige flooring.

Corrugated metal painted a warm Caribbean pink is juxtaposed against the soft green. A stenciled border pattern in teal and coral runs beneath the fluted edge of the canopy. The signage adds touches of a pale dubonnet to the other colors in the palette along with accents of white neon. The pale green color is picked up again on the floor in front of the Fish-Meat display.

DESIGN:
CIP International, Fairfield, OH
Thomas Huff, CEO & Creative Director

"The design approach focuses on the open market feel and is highlighted by the festive colors of the island vegetation." Taking cues and clues from the Caribbean architecture which is primarily designed for an out-of-doors lifestyle, the designers reinterpreted that feeling in the graphics, specifically in the horizontal lines of the window louvres and the parallel lines of the corrugated metal rooftops.

A unique element in the design is the continuous custom floral stencil border. The specialty areas of this almost 60,000 sq. ft. operation, of which 51,000 sq. ft. is devoted to sales, are accentuated by painted corrugated metal "roofs" trimmed with custom craft-

A light green band along with the stenciled border design runs along the off-white perimeter fascia. These, plus the other linear lines on the walls, add "to the expansiveness of the sales area." With variations—but always with the checkerboard motif incorporated—the signage colors are the same.

ed, three dimensional signs finished with checkered patterns. All signs are printed in both English and Spanish—to accommodate the largely Hispanic customer base.

As mentioned previously, this store is a departure from the prototype developed for stores being built in the southeastern and southwestern states. The store's layout, here, emphasizes fresh foods and bountiful perishables. Featured in the Food Pavilion are deli and hot foods, an ethnic bakery, fresh fruit and melon bar, soup and salad bar, service meat and seafood and a genuine Cuban Cafe. Service in the Cafe is available both from inside or outside the store.

The Caribbean-inspired palette is seen everywhere and the appeal to the largely Hispanic customer is readily noted in the Spanish and English signing. The Spanish is particularly evident in the Food Court area.

The Cheese Shop in the Food Court.

As in other Winn Dixie stores, "the lighting and flooring were designed to best display merchandise and accent service departments." Fluorescents provide the general sales area lighting and the perimeter wall decor is illuminated by a cove type wall wash. Color coordinated pendant light fixtures highlight the fresh merchandise in the island displays.

The heritage and tradition of the Latin community is addressed in this specific superstore and the color, texture and theme of the interior design all add up to "an enthusiastic shopping experience."

The "authentic" Cuban Cafe is one of the highlights of the food court area. Here, too, the Caribbean influence is carried through in the corrugated metal awning on the Cafe.

The Pharmacy.

JUMBO HYPERMARKET

Alto Las Condes, Santiago, Chile

The Jumbo Hypermarkets are a leading chain of up-scale grocery — and more — stores which are located prominently throughout Chile and Argentina. The 170,000 sq. ft. superstore — on street level — is actually the third "anchor store" at Alto Los Condes. 130,000 sq. ft. of the space is devoted to sales.

In the Hypermarket the shopper will find, in addition to food and produce, clothing and cosmetics, electronics and appliances, hardware, stationery, film processing, etc. It is like a mall within a mall. "The design strategy was to create a light, fresh and modern atmosphere and in order to humanize and give character to such a large space, we created a series of unique shops."

The powerful facade reflects the bustling boulevard.

One of the shops within the Hypermarket that functions as one of the anchors to the Alto Las Condes Mall.

The Produce department.

DESIGN:
International Design Group, Toronto, ON Canada

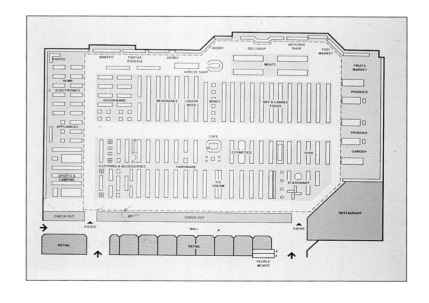

A center island beautifully displays cheese and cheese products.

A warm color scheme was introduced and the perimeter fascias are treated with accent colors and vibrant murals to create a consistent overall backdrop within the various departments. The flooring is white terrazzo tile (12"x12") patterned with subtle shades of gray, sage green, and earthy pink — "to highlight and outline specific departments." Each individual "shop" has its own unique ambience. The Seafood section — "reminiscent of the sea" has blue awnings and a 30' mural depicting various forms of sea food. The walls are covered with aqua/blue tile and the same color accents the refrigeration cases. Decorative props are added such as nets, ship's wheels, oars, and rustic chalk boards used for signage. To cast a warm and flattering light over the products, decorative fixtures with glass shades are hung over the refrigeration units.

In a space as large and as complex as this the lighting plan was important. The designers selected light sources "that enhance the merchandise and provide efficiency and economy." Suspended from the metal truss ceiling are metal halide lamps that provide the

The Fish Counter.

The Wine and Liquor area.

More views of the Jumbo Supermarket. The International Design Group simultaneously created the illusion of being "small" while in fact being so big that it requires 56 check-out counters and two people movers to transport customers from the underground parking lot.

general illumination. Fluorescents and incandescent light sources "with excellent color rendition" were selected for product illumination and some were lowered over the merchandise "to provide a more intimate scale, and direct and add dramatic highlights for the merchandise."

An elaborate signage program was developed that included the aforementioned murals painted on the perimeter fascias over the selling areas. These murals are about 34' long by 4' tall, and they are "stylized in a fashion that adds custom quality, and some use neon to outline and highlight the products — not only making the department stand out even more, but also adding stylishness to the image."

For North American visitors to Jumbo — it is an experience. In a CNN feature broadcast shortly after the Hypermarket opened, Jumbo was described as "no ordinary supermarket." The special achievement of the design was to make a basically uncomfortable environment (a warehouse) into an "atmosphere of upscale luxury" by the use of creative design techniques. The store still maintains a mood of "egalitarian informality, friendliness and warmth."

The Weiner department.

AWARD WINNING DESIGN

analysis

Whether a customer comes to us for a specialty or multiple store project; a remodel or prototype development; the Programmed Products team has experience based on over two decades of analysis, concept development, design, manufacturing, and installation management.

Programmed Products has over twenty years of experience in developing and executing the design plan from concept to completion.

teamwork

The Programmed Products staff is a seasoned team of design and fabrication specialists who have logged thousands of hours collaborating on hundreds of projects.

Our staff works as a team following each project from concept through installation. Our designers, manufacturers and sales consultants communicate daily, coordinating the fine points and objectives of your project.

DESIGN

MANUFACTURING

INSTALLATION

Programmed Products leads the industry in the critical area of full service design. From the store's exterior to fine tuning the interior,

Programmed Products delivers results that immediately help your sales.

No other design firm has been in the comprehensive fabrication and multiple store roll-out business like Programmed Products.

Our in-house manufacturing capabilities result in a distinct cost saving advantage for our clients.

sales

savings

THE PROS

design > from
knowledge
results > from
experience

Create An Effective Retail Environment To Increase Your Sales & Profit

WE PROVIDE INNOVATIVE DESIGN, VALUE ADDED CUSTOM DECOR, AS WELL AS CORPORATE DECOR PACKAGES

When you choose King Design International you're hiring a support team that will work closely with you, your architect and your contractor, to provide a complete package.

From convenience stores to hypermarkets, we work to create a lasting impression that stands the test of time in a highly competitive marketplace.

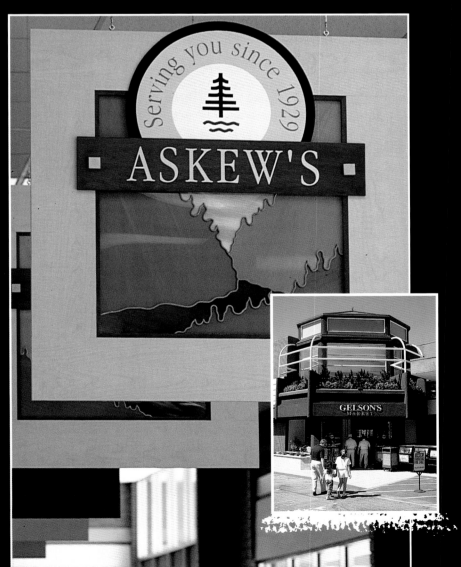

TOTAL TURNKEY SERVICE

Doing it right means attention to detail—
from thumbnail concept through to grand opening.
In between is a unique combination of merchandising expertise
and sophisticated design supported by CAD-based engineering.
CIP takes responsibility. One contact manages your project, overseeing
schedules, manufacturing, quality control, delivery and installation
—and they're all done by experienced CIP people.
The result is an interior that works for you, bringing customers back.
With CIP, you'll go beyond the ordinary…and be confident all the way.

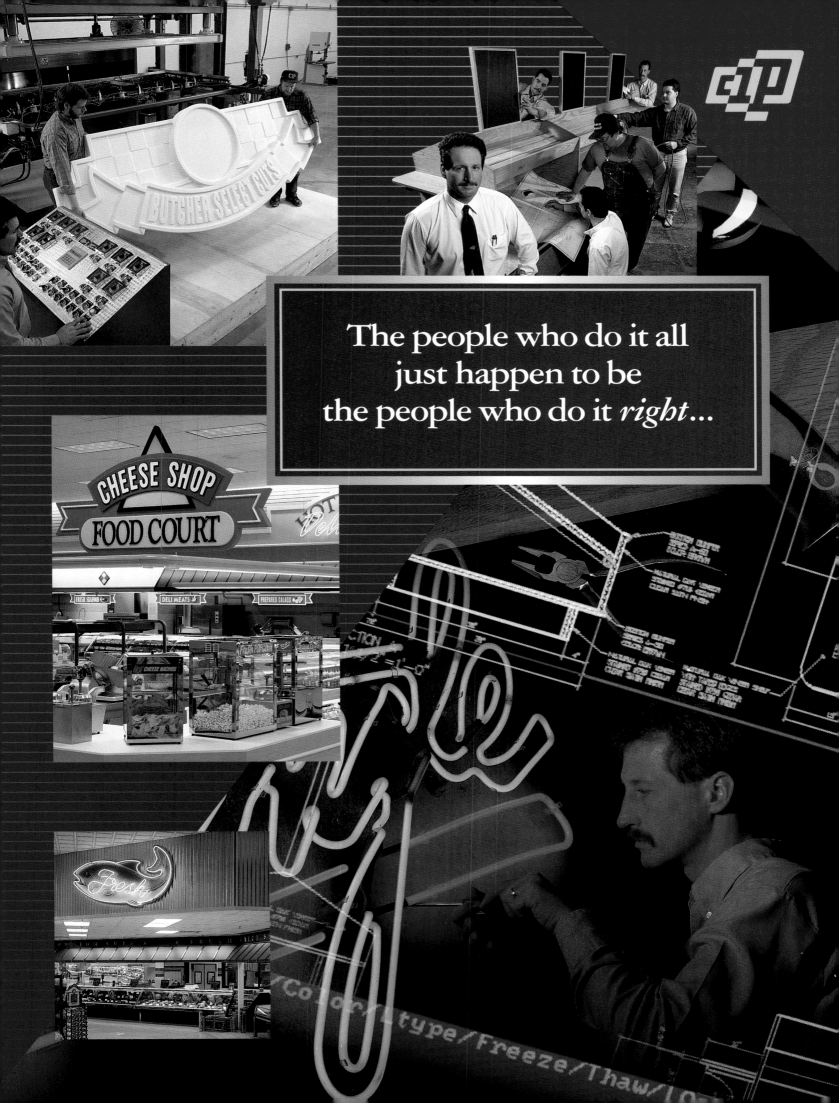

The people who do it all
just happen to be
the people who do it *right*...

The people who do it right
just happen to be
the people who do it *fast*...

LEADING EDGE TECHNOLOGY

Doing it fast means using powerful
computer-aided design and engineering capabilities.
CIP leads the industry in making technology work for you.
Electronic design presentations translate into detail drawings, floor plans,
engineering drawings and specifications—right down to the light bulbs.
You have the opportunity to review every feature and make revisions
before any manufacturing or construction costs are incurred.
It's a process that yields cost-effective—and beautiful—results.
With CIP, you'll go beyond the ordinary...and recognize it when you arrive.

RESULT-DRIVEN DESIGN

Doing it best means creating
a distinctive environment that will entice customers.
And it all begins and ends with design.
CIP uses an integrated approach to create well-planned interiors,
designed to lead shoppers to your profit centers. Along with experience,
CIP brings an understanding of the marketplace—the importance
of timeliness, the need for cost efficiency, and the demand
for overall value with a return on your investment.
With CIP, you'll go beyond the ordinary…and ahead of the competition.

SEAFOOD & MEAT
·S·H·O·P·P·E·S·
Our Finest Selected Cuts

The people who do it fast
just happen to be
the people who do it *best*...

CIP INTERNATIONAL

9575 LeSaint Drive   800-877-7373   INT'L 800-899-9575
Fairfield, Ohio 45014   513-874-9925   FAX 513-874-6246